CoreOS Essentials

HF764181

Develop effective computing networks to deploy your applications and servers using CoreOS

Rimantas Mocevicius

[PACKT] PUBLISHING
open source
community experience distilled
BIRMINGHAM - MUMBAI

CoreOS Essentials

Copyright © 2015 Packt Publishing

All rights reserved. No part of this book may be reproduced, stored in a retrieval system, or transmitted in any form or by any means, without the prior written permission of the publisher, except in the case of brief quotations embedded in critical articles or reviews.

Every effort has been made in the preparation of this book to ensure the accuracy of the information presented. However, the information contained in this book is sold without warranty, either express or implied. Neither the author, nor Packt Publishing, and its dealers and distributors will be held liable for any damages caused or alleged to be caused directly or indirectly by this book.

Packt Publishing has endeavored to provide trademark information about all of the companies and products mentioned in this book by the appropriate use of capitals. However, Packt Publishing cannot guarantee the accuracy of this information.

First published: June 2015

Production reference: 1240615

Published by Packt Publishing Ltd.
Livery Place
35 Livery Street
Birmingham B3 2PB, UK.

ISBN 978-1-78528-394-9

www.packtpub.com

Credits

Author
Rimantas Mocevicius

Reviewers
Brian Harrington
Paul Kirby
Patrick Murray
Melissa Smolensky

Commissioning Editor
Julian Ursell

Acquisition Editor
Usha Iyer

Content Development Editor
Amey Varangaonkar

Technical Editor
Utkarsha S. Kadam

Copy Editor
Vikrant Phadke

Project Coordinator
Bijal Patel

Proofreader
Safis Editing

Indexer
Rekha Nair

Graphics
Abhinash Sahu

Production Coordinator
Aparna Bhagat

Cover Work
Aparna Bhagat

About the Author

Rimantas Mocevicius is an IT professional with over 20 years of experience in Linux. He is a supporter and fan of open source software. His passion for new technologies drives him forward, and he never wants to stop learning about them.

I would like to thank my wife and son for encouraging me to write this book and supporting me all throughout the way until its end.

I also want to say a big thank you to my technical reviewers, Paul Kirby, Brian Harrington, and Patrick Murray, for their invaluable recommendations.

Lots of thanks to the staff at Packt Publishing for guiding me through all of the book writing process and helping make it a nice book.

And of course, a big thank you goes to the CoreOS team for releasing such an amazing Linux-based operating system.

About the Reviewers

Brian 'Redbeard' Harrington is a developer, hacker, and technical writer in the areas of open source development and system administration. He has spent time in both defensive and offensive computing, combined with his readings of classical anarchism, to present new ideas in organizational hierarchies for software development. He has been featured on Al Jazeera as an expert in the field of computer security, and has been seen and heard on Bloomberg Television and National Public Radio. Brian currently resides in Oakland, California, USA. He was formerly the elected president of the HacDC hackerspace.

He is one of the early employees of CoreOS. In true start-up terms, this means that he has done everything from taking out the trash to racking servers and stepping on site with customers. He has previously worked with Red Hat, the US Census Bureau, and other organizations, chopping wood and carrying water to keep the Internet running.

Thank you to Holly. I'll always strive to make you proud.

Patrick Murray is a senior software engineer at Cisco Systems. He has been working in the Silicon Valley since 2008. He completed his education in computer engineering from Michigan Technological University in Houghton, Michigan, USA. His primary technology interests are cloud deployment and orchestration, distributed systems, NoSQL, and big data.

I would like to thank my beautiful newborn daughter, Amelia, and my wife, Xian, for their support and for letting me find the time to work as a reviewer.

Melissa Smolensky is the director of marketing at CoreOS and oversees all the marketing activities there. She is passionate about start-ups, the future of technology, and how technology is changing the way we consume and interact with media.

www.PacktPub.com

Support files, eBooks, discount offers, and more

For support files and downloads related to your book, please visit `www.PacktPub.com`.

Did you know that Packt offers eBook versions of every book published, with PDF and ePub files available? You can upgrade to the eBook version at `www.PacktPub.com` and as a print book customer, you are entitled to a discount on the eBook copy. Get in touch with us at `service@packtpub.com` for more details.

At `www.PacktPub.com`, you can also read a collection of free technical articles, sign up for a range of free newsletters and receive exclusive discounts and offers on Packt books and eBooks.

PACKTLIB™

`https://www2.packtpub.com/books/subscription/packtlib`

Do you need instant solutions to your IT questions? PacktLib is Packt's online digital book library. Here, you can search, access, and read Packt's entire library of books.

Why subscribe?

- Fully searchable across every book published by Packt
- Copy and paste, print, and bookmark content
- On demand and accessible via a web browser

Free access for Packt account holders

If you have an account with Packt at `www.PacktPub.com`, you can use this to access PacktLib today and view 9 entirely free books. Simply use your login credentials for immediate access.

Table of Contents

Preface

CoreOS is a new breed of the Linux operating system and is optimized to run Linux containers, such as Docker and rkt. It has a fully automated update system, no package manager, and a fully clustered architecture.

Whether you are a Linux expert or just a beginner with some knowledge of Linux, this book will provide you with step-by-step instructions on installing and configuring CoreOS servers as well as building development and production environments. You will be introduced to the new CoreOS rkt Application Containers runtime engine and Google's Kubernetes system, which allows you to manage a cluster of Linux containers as a single system.

What this book covers

Chapter 1, CoreOS – Overview and Installation, contains a brief CoreOS overview what CoreOS is about.

Chapter 2, Getting Started with etcd, explains what etcd is and what it can be used for.

Chapter 3, Getting Started with systemd and fleet, covers an overview of systemd. This chapter tells you what fleet is and how to use it to deploy Docker containers.

Chapter 4, Managing Clusters, is a guide to setting up and managing a cluster.

Chapter 5, Building a Development Environment, shows you how to set up the CoreOS development environment to test your Application Containers.

Chapter 6, Building a Deployment Setup, helps you set up code deployment, the Docker image builder, and the private Docker registry.

Chapter 7, Building a Production Cluster, explains the setup of the CoreOS production cluster on the cloud.

Chapter 8, Introducing CoreUpdate and Container/Enterprise Registry, has an overview of free and paid CoreOS services.

Chapter 9, Introduction to CoreOS rkt, tells you what rkt is and how to use it.

Chapter 10, Introduction to Kubernetes, teaches you how to set up and use Kubernetes.

What you need for this book

For this book, you will need a Linux-powered system or an Apple Mac, and a Google Cloud account to run the examples covered. You will also require the latest versions of VirtualBox and Vagrant to run the scripts.

Who this book is for

This book will benefit any Linux/Unix system administrator. Any person with even a basic knowledge of Linux/Unix will have an advantage when using this book.

This book is also for system engineers and system administrators who are already experienced with network virtualization and want to understand how CoreOS can be used to develop computing networks for the deployment of applications and servers. They must have a proper knowledge of the Linux operating system and Application Containers, and it is better if they have used a Linux distribution for the purpose of development or administration before.

Conventions

In this book, you will find a number of styles of text that distinguish between different kinds of information. Here are some examples of these styles, and an explanation of their meaning.

Code words in text are shown as follows: "We can include other contexts through the use of the `include` directive."

A block of code is set as follows:

```
etcd2:
  name: core-01
  initial-advertise-peer-urls: http://$private_ipv4:2380
  listen-peer-urls:
    http://$private_ipv4:2380,http://$private_ipv4:7001
  initial-cluster-token: core-01_etcd
  initial-cluster: core-01=http://$private_ipv4:2380
  initial-cluster-state: new
  advertise-client-urls:
    http://$public_ipv4:2379,http://$public_ipv4:4001
  listen-client-urls: http://0.0.0.0:2379,http://0.0.0.0:4001
fleet:
```

Any command-line input or output is written as follows:

```
$ git clone https://github.com/coreos/coreos-vagrant/
```

New terms and **important words** are shown in bold. Words that you see on the screen, in menus or dialog boxes for example, appear in the text like this: "We should see this output in the **Terminal** window."

> Warnings or important notes appear in a box like this.

> Tips and tricks appear like this.

Reader feedback

Feedback from our readers is always welcome. Let us know what you think about this book—what you liked or disliked. Reader feedback is important for us as it helps us develop titles that you will really get the most out of.

To send us general feedback, simply e-mail `feedback@packtpub.com` and mention the book's title in the subject of your message.

If there is a topic that you have expertise in and you are interested in either writing or contributing to a book, see our author guide at `www.packtpub.com/authors`.

Customer support

Now that you are the proud owner of a Packt book, we have a number of things to help you to get the most from your purchase.

Downloading the example code

You can download the example code files from your account at `http://www.packtpub.com` for all the Packt Publishing books you have purchased. If you purchased this book elsewhere, you can visit `http://www.packtpub.com/support` and register to have the files e-mailed directly to you.

Errata

Although we have taken every care to ensure the accuracy of our content, mistakes do happen. If you find a mistake in one of our books—maybe a mistake in the text or the code—we would be grateful if you could report this to us. By doing so, you can save other readers from frustration and help us improve subsequent versions of this book. If you find any errata, please report them by visiting `http://www.packtpub.com/submit-errata`, selecting your book, clicking on the **Errata Submission Form** link, and entering the details of your errata. Once your errata are verified, your submission will be accepted and the errata will be uploaded to our website or added to any list of existing errata under the Errata section of that title.

To view the previously submitted errata, go to `https://www.packtpub.com/books/content/support` and enter the name of the book in the search field. The required information will appear under the **Errata** section.

Piracy

Piracy of copyrighted material on the Internet is an ongoing problem across all media. At Packt, we take the protection of our copyright and licenses very seriously. If you come across any illegal copies of our works in any form on the Internet, please provide us with the location address or website name immediately so that we can pursue a remedy.

We appreciate your help in protecting our authors, and our ability to bring you valuable content.

Questions

You can contact us at `questions@packtpub.com` if you are having a problem with any aspect of the book, and we will do our best to address it.

1

CoreOS – Overview and Installation

CoreOS is often described as Linux for massive server deployments, but it can also run easily as a single host on bare-metal, cloud servers, and as a virtual machine on your computer as well. It is designed to run application containers as `docker` and `rkt`, and you will learn about its main features later in this book.

This book is a practical, example-driven guide to help you learn about the essentials of the CoreOS Linux operating system. We assume that you have experience with VirtualBox, Vagrant, Git, Bash shell scripting and the command line (terminal on UNIX-like computers), and you have already installed VirtualBox, Vagrant, and git on your Mac OS X or Linux computer, which will be needed for the first chapters. As for a cloud installation, we will use Google Cloud's Compute Engine instances.

By the end of this book, you will hopefully be familiar with setting up CoreOS on your laptop or desktop, and on the cloud. You will learn how to set up a local computer development machine and a cluster on a local computer and in the cloud. Also, we will cover `etcd`, `systemd`, `fleet`, cluster management, deployment setup, and production clusters.

Also, the last chapter will introduce Google Kubernetes. This is an open source orchestration system for `docker` and `rkt` containers and allows to manage them as a single system on on compute clusters.

In this chapter, you will learn how CoreOS works and how to carry out a basic CoreOS installation on your laptop or desktop with the help of VirtualBox and Vagrant.

We will basically cover two topics in this chapter:

- An overview of CoreOS
- Installing the CoreOS virtual machine

An overview of CoreOS

CoreOS is a minimal Linux operation system built to run `docker` and `rkt` containers (application containers). By default, it is designed to build powerful and easily manageable server clusters. It provides automatic, very reliable, and stable updates to all machines, which takes away a big maintenance headache from `sysadmins`. And, by running everything in application containers, such setup allows you to very easily scale servers and applications, replace faulty servers in a fraction of a second, and so on.

How CoreOS works

CoreOS has no package manager, so everything needs to be installed and used via `docker` containers. Moreover, it is 40 percent more efficient in RAM usage than an average Linux installation, as shown in this diagram:

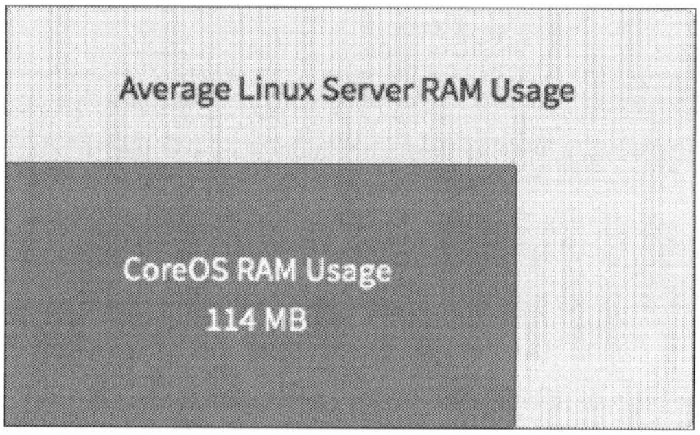

CoreOS utilizes an active/passive dual-partition scheme to update itself as a single unit, instead of using a package-by-package method. Its root partition is read-only and changes only when an update is applied. If the update is unsuccessful during reboot time, then it rolls back to the previous boot partition. The following image shows OS updated gets applied to partition B (passive) and after reboot it becomes the active to boot from.

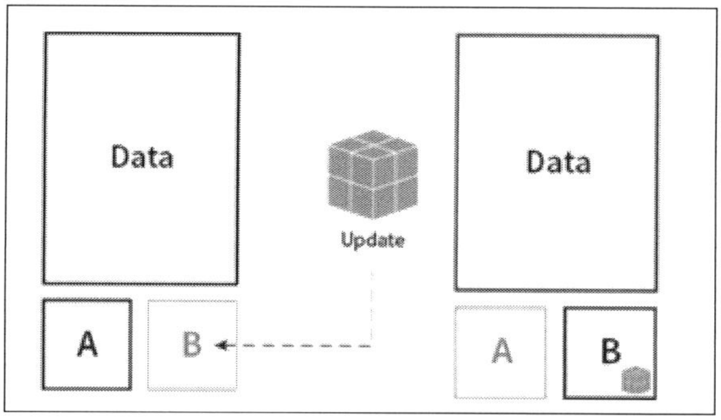

The `docker` and `rkt` containers run as applications on CoreOS. Containers can provide very good flexibility for application packaging and can start very quickly—in a matter of milliseconds. The following image shows the simplicity of CoreOS. Bottom part is Linux OS, the second level is `etcd/fleet` with docker daemon and the top level are running containers on the server.

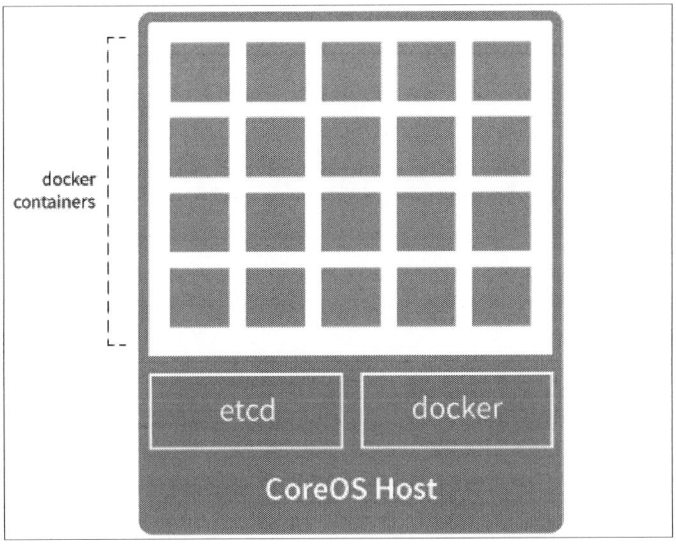

By default, CoreOS is designed to work in a clustered form, but it also works very well as a single host. It is very easy to control and run application containers across cluster machines with `fleet` and use the `etcd` service discovery to connect them as it shown in the following image.

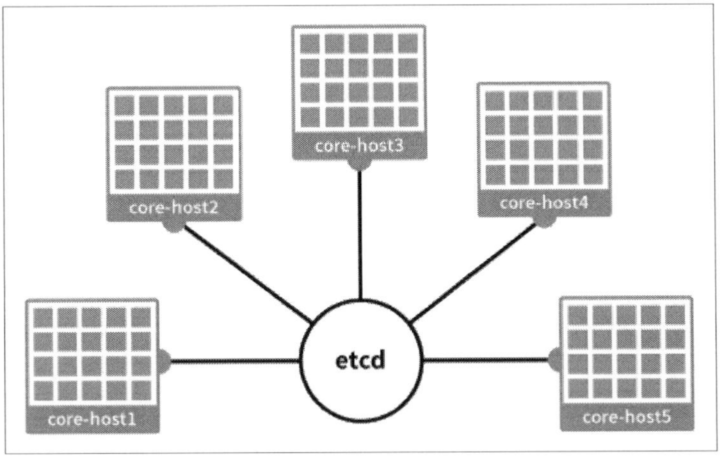

CoreOS can be deployed easily on all major cloud providers, for example, Google Cloud, Amazon Web Services, Digital Ocean, and so on. It runs very well on bare-metal servers as well. Moreover, it can be easily installed on a laptop or desktop with Linux, Mac OS X, or Windows via Vagrant, with VirtualBox or VMware virtual machine support.

This short overview should throw some light on what CoreOS is about and what it can do. Let's now move on to the real stuff and install CoreOS on to our laptop or desktop machine.

Installing the CoreOS virtual machine

To use the CoreOS virtual machine, you need to have VirtualBox, Vagrant, and git installed on your computer.

In the following examples, we will install CoreOS on our local computer, which will serve as a virtual machine on VirtualBox.

Okay, let's get started!

Cloning the coreos-vagrant GitHub project

Let's clone this project and get it running.

In your terminal (from now on, we will use just the terminal phrase and use `$` to label the terminal prompt), type the following command:

```
$ git clone https://github.com/coreos/coreos-vagrant/
```

This will clone from the GitHub repository to the `coreos-vagrant` folder on your computer.

Working with cloud-config

To start even a single host, we need to provide some `config` parameters in the `cloud-config` format via the user data file.

In your terminal, type this:

```
$ cd coreos-vagrant
$ mv user-data.sample user-data
```

The user data should have content like this (the `coreos-vagrant` Github repository is constantly changing, so you might see a bit of different content when you clone the repository):

```
#cloud-config
coreos:
  etcd2:
    #generate a new token for each unique cluster from
      https://discovery.etcd.io/new
    #discovery: https://discovery.etcd.io/<token>
    # multi-region and multi-cloud deployments need to use
      $public_ipv4
    advertise-client-urls: http://$public_ipv4:2379
    initial-advertise-peer-urls: http://$private_ipv4:2380
    # listen on both the official ports and the legacy ports
    # legacy ports can be omitted if your application doesn't
      depend on them
    listen-client-urls: http://0.0.0.0:2379,http://0.0.0.0:4001
    listen-peer-urls:
      http://$private_ipv4:2380,http://$private_ipv4:7001
  fleet:
    public-ip: $public_ipv4
  flannel:
    interface: $public_ipv4
  units:
    - name: etcd2.service
      command: start
    - name: fleet.service
      command: start
    - name: docker-tcp.socket
      command: start
      enable: true
      content: |
        [Unit]
        Description=Docker Socket for the API

        [Socket]
        ListenStream=2375
        Service=docker.service
        BindIPv6Only=both
        [Install]
        WantedBy=sockets.target
```

Replace the text between the `etcd2:` and `fleet:` lines to look this:

```
etcd2:
  name: core-01
  initial-advertise-peer-urls: http://$private_ipv4:2380
  listen-peer-urls:
    http://$private_ipv4:2380,http://$private_ipv4:7001
  initial-cluster-token: core-01_etcd
  initial-cluster: core-01=http://$private_ipv4:2380
  initial-cluster-state: new
  advertise-client-urls:
    http://$public_ipv4:2379,http://$public_ipv4:4001
  listen-client-urls: http://0.0.0.0:2379,http://0.0.0.0:4001
fleet:
```

> You can also download the latest `user-data` file from `https://github.com/rimusz/coreos-essentials-book/blob/master/Chapter1/user-data`.

This should be enough to bootstrap a single-host CoreOS VM with `etcd`, `fleet`, and `docker` running there.

We will cover `cloud-config`, `etcd` and `fleet` in more detail in later chapters.

Startup and SSH

It's now time to boot our CoreOS VM and log in to its console using `ssh`.

Let's boot our first CoreOS VM host. To do so, using the terminal, type the following command:

```
$ vagrant up
```

This will trigger vagrant to download the latest CoreOS alpha (this is the default channel set in the `config.rb` file, and it can easily be changed to beta, or stable) channel image and the `lunch` VM instance.

You should see something like this as the output in your terminal:

```
Bringing machine 'core-01' up with 'virtualbox' provider...
==> core-01: Box 'coreos-alpha' could not be found. Attempting to find and install...
    core-01: Box Provider: virtualbox
    core-01: Box Version: >= 308.0.1
==> core-01: Loading metadata for box 'http://alpha.release.core-os.net/amd64-usr/current/coreos_production_vagrant.json'
    core-01: URL: http://alpha.release.core-os.net/amd64-usr/current/coreos_production_vagrant.json
==> core-01: Adding box 'coreos-alpha' (v681.0.0) for provider: virtualbox
    core-01: Downloading: http://alpha.release.core-os.net/amd64-usr/681.0.0/coreos_production_vagrant.box
    core-01: Calculating and comparing box checksum...
==> core-01: Successfully added box 'coreos-alpha' (v681.0.0) for 'virtualbox'!
==> core-01: Importing base box 'coreos-alpha'...
==> core-01: Matching MAC address for NAT networking...
==> core-01: Checking if box 'coreos-alpha' is up to date...
==> core-01: Setting the name of the VM: coreos-vagrant_core-01_1431638846664_68246
==> core-01: Clearing any previously set network interfaces...
==> core-01: Preparing network interfaces based on configuration...
    core-01: Adapter 1: nat
    core-01: Adapter 2: hostonly
==> core-01: Forwarding ports...
    core-01: 22 => 2222 (adapter 1)
==> core-01: Running 'pre-boot' VM customizations...
==> core-01: Booting VM...
==> core-01: Waiting for machine to boot. This may take a few minutes...
    core-01: SSH address: 127.0.0.1:2222
    core-01: SSH username: core
    core-01: SSH auth method: private key
    core-01: Warning: Connection timeout. Retrying...
==> core-01: Machine booted and ready!
==> core-01: Setting hostname...
==> core-01: Configuring and enabling network interfaces...
==> core-01: Running provisioner: file...
==> core-01: Running provisioner: shell...
    core-01: Running: inline script
```

CoreOS VM has booted up, so let's open the `ssh` connection to our new VM using the following command:

```
$ vagrant ssh
```

It should show something like this:

```
CoreOS alpha (some version)
core@core-01 ~ $
```

> **Downloading the example code**
>
> You can download the example code files from your account at `http://www.packtpub.com` for all the Packt Publishing books you have purchased. If you purchased this book elsewhere, you can visit `http://www.packtpub.com/support` and register to have the files e-mailed directly to you.

Perfect! Let's verify that `etcd`, `fleet`, and `docker` are running there. Here are the commands required and the corresponding screenshots of the output:

```
$ systemctl status etcd2
```

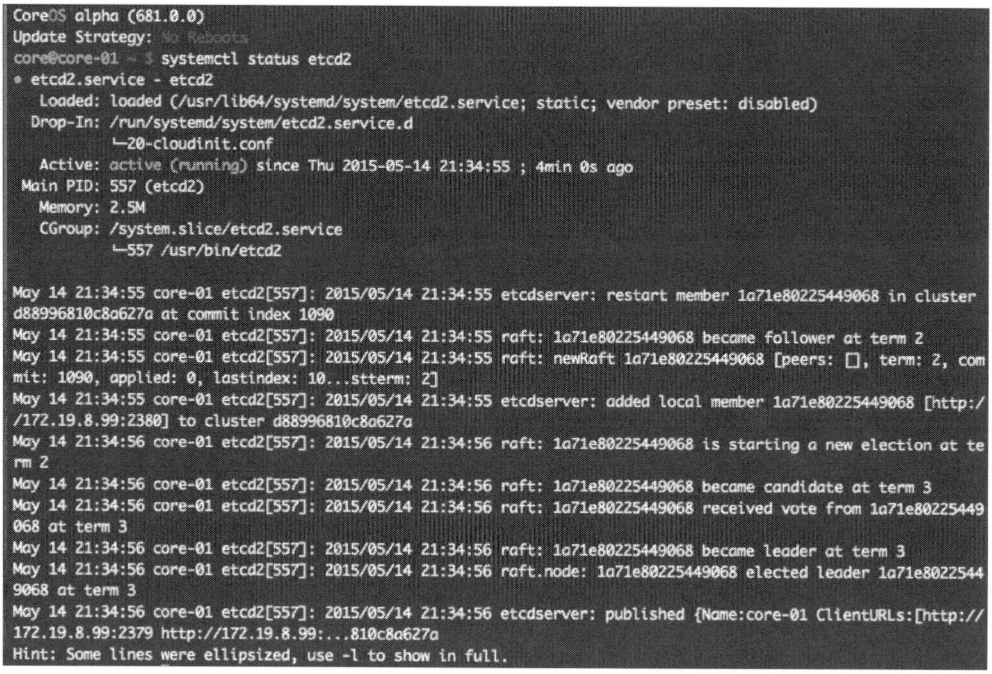

```
CoreOS alpha (681.0.0)
Update Strategy: No Reboots
core@core-01 ~ $ systemctl status etcd2
● etcd2.service - etcd2
   Loaded: loaded (/usr/lib64/systemd/system/etcd2.service; static; vendor preset: disabled)
  Drop-In: /run/systemd/system/etcd2.service.d
           └─20-cloudinit.conf
   Active: active (running) since Thu 2015-05-14 21:34:55 ; 4min 0s ago
 Main PID: 557 (etcd2)
   Memory: 2.5M
   CGroup: /system.slice/etcd2.service
           └─557 /usr/bin/etcd2

May 14 21:34:55 core-01 etcd2[557]: 2015/05/14 21:34:55 etcdserver: restart member 1a71e80225449068 in cluster d88996810c8a627a at commit index 1090
May 14 21:34:55 core-01 etcd2[557]: 2015/05/14 21:34:55 raft: 1a71e80225449068 became follower at term 2
May 14 21:34:55 core-01 etcd2[557]: 2015/05/14 21:34:55 raft: newRaft 1a71e80225449068 [peers: [], term: 2, commit: 1090, applied: 0, lastindex: 10...stterm: 2]
May 14 21:34:55 core-01 etcd2[557]: 2015/05/14 21:34:55 etcdserver: added local member 1a71e80225449068 [http://172.19.8.99:2380] to cluster d88996810c8a627a
May 14 21:34:56 core-01 etcd2[557]: 2015/05/14 21:34:56 raft: 1a71e80225449068 is starting a new election at term 2
May 14 21:34:56 core-01 etcd2[557]: 2015/05/14 21:34:56 raft: 1a71e80225449068 became candidate at term 3
May 14 21:34:56 core-01 etcd2[557]: 2015/05/14 21:34:56 raft: 1a71e80225449068 received vote from 1a71e80225449068 at term 3
May 14 21:34:56 core-01 etcd2[557]: 2015/05/14 21:34:56 raft: 1a71e80225449068 became leader at term 3
May 14 21:34:56 core-01 etcd2[557]: 2015/05/14 21:34:56 raft.node: 1a71e80225449068 elected leader 1a71e80225449068 at term 3
May 14 21:34:56 core-01 etcd2[557]: 2015/05/14 21:34:56 etcdserver: published {Name:core-01 ClientURLs:[http://172.19.8.99:2379 http://172.19.8.99:...810c8a627a
Hint: Some lines were ellipsized, use -l to show in full.
```

To check the status of `fleet`, type this:

```
$ systemctl status fleet
```

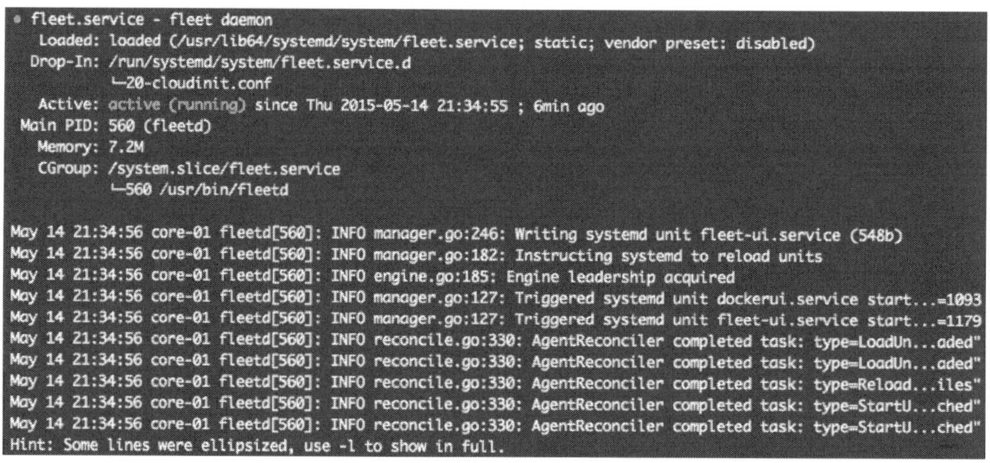

```
● fleet.service - fleet daemon
   Loaded: loaded (/usr/lib64/systemd/system/fleet.service; static; vendor preset: disabled)
  Drop-In: /run/systemd/system/fleet.service.d
           └─20-cloudinit.conf
   Active: active (running) since Thu 2015-05-14 21:34:55 ; 6min ago
 Main PID: 560 (fleetd)
   Memory: 7.2M
   CGroup: /system.slice/fleet.service
           └─560 /usr/bin/fleetd

May 14 21:34:56 core-01 fleetd[560]: INFO manager.go:246: Writing systemd unit fleet-ui.service (548b)
May 14 21:34:56 core-01 fleetd[560]: INFO manager.go:182: Instructing systemd to reload units
May 14 21:34:56 core-01 fleetd[560]: INFO engine.go:185: Engine leadership acquired
May 14 21:34:56 core-01 fleetd[560]: INFO manager.go:127: Triggered systemd unit dockerui.service start...=1093
May 14 21:34:56 core-01 fleetd[560]: INFO manager.go:127: Triggered systemd unit fleet-ui.service start...=1179
May 14 21:34:56 core-01 fleetd[560]: INFO reconcile.go:330: AgentReconciler completed task: type=LoadUn...aded"
May 14 21:34:56 core-01 fleetd[560]: INFO reconcile.go:330: AgentReconciler completed task: type=LoadUn...aded"
May 14 21:34:56 core-01 fleetd[560]: INFO reconcile.go:330: AgentReconciler completed task: type=Reload...iles"
May 14 21:34:56 core-01 fleetd[560]: INFO reconcile.go:330: AgentReconciler completed task: type=StartU...ched"
May 14 21:34:56 core-01 fleetd[560]: INFO reconcile.go:330: AgentReconciler completed task: type=StartU...ched"
Hint: Some lines were ellipsized, use -l to show in full.
```

To check the status of `docker`, type the following command:

```
$ docker version
```

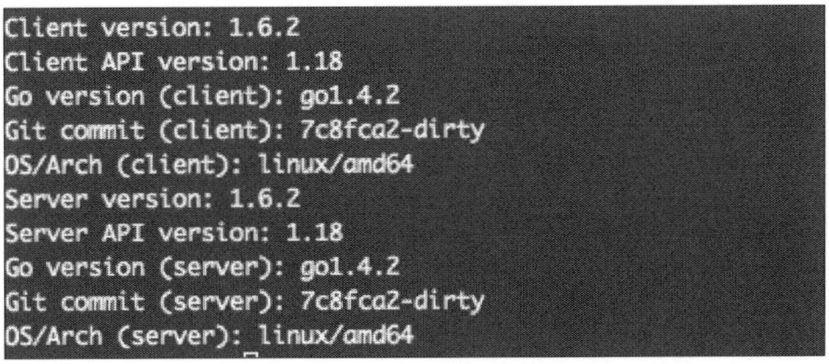

Lovely! Everything looks fine. Thus, we've got our first CoreOS VM up and running in VirtualBox.

Summary

In this chapter, we saw what CoreOS is and how it is installed. We covered a simple CoreOS installation on a local computer with the help of Vagrant and VirtualBox, and checked whether `etcd`, `fleet`, and `docker` are running there.

You will continue to explore and learn about all CoreOS services in more detail in the upcoming chapters.

2

Getting Started with etcd

In this chapter, we will cover `etcd`, CoreOS's central hub of services, which provides a reliable way of storing shared data across cluster machines and monitoring it.

For testing, we will use our already installed CoreOS VM from the previous chapter. In this chapter, we will cover the following topics:

- Introducing `etcd`
- Reading and writing to `etcd` from the host machine
- Reading and writing from an application container
- Watching changes in `etcd`
- TTL (Time to Live) examples
- Use cases of `etcd`

Introducing etcd

The `etcd` function is an open source distributed key value store on a computer network where information is stored on more than one node and data is replicated using the Raft consensus algorithm. The `etcd` function is used to store the CoreOS cluster service discovery and the shared configuration.

The configuration is stored in the write-ahead log and includes the cluster member ID, cluster ID and cluster configuration, and is accessible by all cluster members.

The `etcd` function runs on each cluster's central services role machine, and gracefully handles master election during network partitions and in the event of a loss of the current master.

Reading and writing to etcd from the host machine

You are going to learn how read and write to `ectd` from the host machine. We will use both the `etcdctl` and `curl` examples here.

Logging in to the host

To log in to CoreOS VM, follow these steps:

1. Boot the CoreOS VM installed in the first chapter. In your terminal, type this:

   ```
   $ cdcoreos-vagrant
   $ vagrant up
   ```

2. We need to log in to the host via `ssh`:

   ```
   $ vagrant ssh
   ```

Reading and writing to ectd

Let's read and write to `etcd` using `etcdctl`. So, perform these steps:

1. Set a `message1` key with `etcdctl` with `Book1` as the value:

   ```
   $ etcdctl set /message1 Book1
   Book1 (we got respond for our successful write to etcd)
   ```

2. Now, let's read the key value to double-check whether everything is fine there:

   ```
   $ etcdctl get /message1
   Book1
   Perfect!
   ```

3. Next, let's try to do the same using `curl` via an HTTP-based API. The `curl` function is handy for accessing `etcd` from any place from where you have access to an `etcd` cluster but don't want/need to use the `etcdctl` client:

   ```
   $ curl -L -X PUT http://127.0.0.1:2379/v2/keys/message2 -d
   value="Book2"
   {"action":"set","key":"/message2","prevValue":"Book1","value":"Boo
   k2","index":13371}
   ```

Let's read it:

```
$ curl -L http://127.0.0.1:2379/v2/keys/message2
{"action":"get","node":{"key":"/message2","value":"Book2","modifie
dIndex":13371,"createdIndex":13371}}
```

Using the HTTP-based `etcd` API means that `etcd` can be read from and written to by client applications without the need to interact with the command line.

4. Now, if we want to delete the key-value pair, we type the following command:

   ```
   $ etcdctl rm /message1
   $ curl -L -X DELETE http://127.0.0.1:2379/v2/keys/message2
   ```

5. Also, we can add a key value pair to a directory, as directories are created automatically when a key is placed inside. We only need one command to put a key inside a directory:

   ```
   $ etcdctl set /foo-directory/foo-key somekey
   ```

6. Let's now check the directory's content:

   ```
   $ etcdctl ls /foo-directory -recursive
   /foo-directory/foo-key
   ```

7. Finally, we get the key value from the directory by typing:

   ```
   $ etcdctl get /foo-directory/foo-key
   somekey
   ```

Reading and writing from the application container

Usually, application containers (this is a general term for `docker`, `rkt`, and other types of containers) do not have `etcdctl` or even `curl` installed by default. Installing `curl` is much easier than installing `etcdctl`.

For our example, we will use the Alpine Linux docker image, which is very small in size and will not take much time to pull from the `docker` registry:

1. Firstly, we need to check the `docker0` interface IP, which we will use with `curl`:

   ```
   $ echo"$(ifconfig docker0 | awk'/\<inet\>/ { print $2}'):2379"
   10.1.42.1:2379
   ```

2. Let's run the `docker` container with a `bash` shell:

   ```
   $ docker run -it alpine ash
   ```

   We should see something like this in Command Prompt:`/ #`.

3. As `curl` is not installed by default on Alpine Linux, we need to install it:

   ```
   $ apk update&&apk add curl
   $ curl -L http://10.1.42.1:2379/v2/keys/
   {"action":"get","node":{"key":"/","dir":true,"nodes":[{"key":"/
   coreos.com","dir":true,"modifiedIndex":3,"createdIndex":3}]}}
   ```

4. Repeat steps 3 and 4 from the previous subtopic so that you understand that no matter where you are connecting to `etcd` from, `curl` still works in the same way.

5. Press *Ctrl +D* to exit from the `docker` container.

Watching changes in etcd

This time, let's watch the key changes in `etcd`. Watching key changes is useful when we have, for example, one `fleet` unit with `nginx` writing its port to `etcd`, and another reverse proxy application watching for changes and updating its configuration:

1. We need to create a directory in `etcd` first:

   ```
   $ etcdctlmkdir /foo-data
   ```

2. Next, we watch for changes in this directory:

   ```
   $ etcdctl watch /foo-data--recursive
   ```

3. Now open another CoreOS shell in a new terminal window:

   ```
   $ cdcoreos-vagrant
   $ vagrantssh
   ```

4. We add a new key to the `/foo-data` directory:

   ```
   $ etcdctl set /foo-data/Book is_cool
   ```

5. In the first terminal, we should see a notification saying that the key was changed:

   ```
   is_cool
   ```

TTL (time to live) examples

Sometimes, it is handy to put a **time to live** (**TTL**) for a key to expire in a certain amount of time. This is useful, for example, in the case of watching a key with a 60 second TTL, from a reverse proxy. So, if the `nginx fleet` service has not updated the key, it will expire in 60 seconds and will be removed from `etcd`. Then the reverse proxy checks for it and does not find it. Hence, it will remove the `nginx` service from `config`.

Let's set a TTL of 30 seconds in this example:

1. Type this in a terminal:

   ```
   $ etcdctl set /foo "I'm Expiring in 30 sec" --ttl 30
   I'm Expiring in 30 sec
   ```

2. Verify that the key is still there:

   ```
   $ etcdctl get /foo
   I'm Expiring in 30 sec
   ```

3. Check again after 30 seconds :

   ```
   $ etcdctl get /foo
   ```

4. If your requested key has already expired, you will be returned `Error: 100`:

   ```
   Error: 100: Key not found (/foo) [17053]
   ```

This time the key got deleted by `etcd` because we put a TTL of 30 seconds for it.

> TTL is very handy to use to communicate between the different services using `etcd` as the checking point.

Use cases of etcd

Application containers running on worker nodes with `etcd` in proxy mode can read and write to an `etcd` cluster.

Very common `etcd` use cases are as follows: storing database connection settings, cache settings, and shared settings. For example, the Vulcand proxy server (`http://vulcanproxy.com/`) uses `etcd` to store web host connection details, and it becomes available for all cluster-connected worker machines. Another example could be to store a database password for MySQL and retrieve it when running an application container.

We will cover more details about cluster setup, central services, and worker role machines in the upcoming chapters.

Summary

In this short chapter, we covered the basics of `etcd` and how to read and write to `etcd`, watch for changes in `etcd`, and use TTL for `etcd` keys.

In the next chapter, you will learn how to use the `systemd` and `fleet` units.

3
Getting Started with systemd and fleet

In this chapter, we will cover the basics of systemd and `fleet`, which includes system unit files. We will demonstrate how to use a `fleet` to launch Docker containers.

We will cover the following topics in this chapter:

- Getting started with `systemd`
- Getting started with `fleet`

Getting started with systemd

You are going to learn what `systemd` is about and how to use `systemctl` to control `systemd` units.

An overview of systemd

The `systemd` is an init system used by CoreOS for starting, stopping, and managing processes.

Basically, it is a system and service manager for CoreOS. On CoreOS, `systemd` will be used almost exclusively to manage the life cycle of Docker containers. The `systemd` records initialization instructions for each process in the unit file, which has many types, but we will mainly be covering the "service" unit file, as covering all of them is beyond the scope for this book.

The systemd unit files

The `systemd` records initialization instructions/properties for each process in the "service" unit file we want to run. On CoreOS, unit files installed by the user manually or via cloud-init are placed at `/etc/systemd/system`, which is a read-write filesystem, as a large part of CoreOS has only read-only access. Units curated by the CoreOS team are placed in `/usr/lib64/system/system`, and ephemeral units, which exist for the runtime of a single boot, are located at `/run/system/system`. This is really good to know for debugging `fleet` services.

Okay, let's create a unit file to test `systemd`:

1. Boot your CoreOS VM installed in the first chapter and log in to the host via `ssh`.
2. Let's create a simple unit file, `hello.service`:

   ```
   $ sudo vi /etc/systemd/system/hello.service
   ```

   Press *I* and copy and paste the following text (or use the provided example file, `hello.service`):

   ```
   [Unit]
   Description=HelloWorld
   # this unit will only start after docker.service
   After=docker.service
   Requires=docker.service

   [Service]
   TimeoutStartSec=0
   # busybox image will be pulled from docker public registry
   ExecStartPre=/usr/bin/docker pull busybox
   # we use rm just in case the container with the name "busybox1" is
   left
   ExecStartPre=-/usr/bin/docker rm busybox1
   # we start docker container
   ExecStart=/usr/bin/docker run --rm --name busybox1 busybox /bin/sh
   -c "while true; do echo Hello World; sleep 1; done"
   # we stop docker container when systemctl stop is used
   ExecStop=/usr/bin/docker stop busybox1

   [Install]
   WantedBy=multi-user.target
   ```

3. Press *Esc* and then type `:wq` to save the file.

4. To start the new unit, run this command:

   $ sudo systemctl enable /etc/systemd/system/hello.service

   Created a symlink from `/etc/systemd/system/multi-user.target.wants/hello.service` to `/etc/systemd/system/hello.service`.

   $ sudo systemctl start hello.service

5. Let's verify that the `hello.service` unit got started:

   $ journalctl -f -u hello.service

   # You should see the unit's output similar to this:

```
-- Logs begin at Thu 2015-05-14 21:52:42 . --
May 26 22:03:05 core-01 docker[830]: Hello World
May 26 22:03:06 core-01 docker[830]: Hello World
May 26 22:03:07 core-01 docker[830]: Hello World
May 26 22:03:08 core-01 docker[830]: Hello World
May 26 22:03:09 core-01 docker[830]: Hello World
May 26 22:03:10 core-01 docker[830]: Hello World
May 26 22:03:11 core-01 docker[830]: Hello World
May 26 22:03:12 core-01 docker[830]: Hello World
May 26 22:03:13 core-01 docker[830]: Hello World
May 26 22:03:14 core-01 docker[830]: Hello World
May 26 22:03:15 core-01 docker[830]: Hello World
May 26 22:03:16 core-01 docker[830]: Hello World
May 26 22:03:17 core-01 docker[830]: Hello World
```

Also, you can check out the list of containers running with `docker ps`.

In the previous steps, we created the `hello.service` system unit, enabled and started it, and checked that unit's log file with `journalctl`.

> To read about more advanced use of the `systemd` unit files, go to `https://coreos.com/docs/launching-containers/launching/getting-started-with-systemd`.

An overview of systemctl

The `systemctl` is used to control and provide an introspection of the state of the `systemd` system and its units.

It is like your interface to a system (similar to `supervisord/supervisordctl` from other Linux distribution), as all processes on a single machine are started and managed by `systemd`, which includes `docker` containers too.

We have already used it in the preceding example to enable and start the `hello.service` unit.

The following are some useful `systemctl` commands, with their purposes:

1. Checking the status of the unit:

   `$ sudo systemctl status hello.service`

   You should see a similar output as follows:

```
● hello.service - HelloWorld
   Loaded: loaded (/etc/systemd/system/hello.service; enabled; vendor preset: disabled)
   Active: active (running) since Tue 2015-05-26 22:03:02 ; 3min 3s ago
  Process: 824 ExecStartPre=/usr/bin/docker rm busybox1 (code=exited, status=1/FAILURE)
  Process: 737 ExecStartPre=/usr/bin/docker pull busybox (code=exited, status=0/SUCCESS
 Main PID: 830 (docker)
   Memory: 11.0M
   CGroup: /system.slice/hello.service
           └─830 /usr/bin/docker run --rm --name busybox1 busybox /bin/sh -c while true
do echo Hello World; sleep 1; done

May 26 22:05:55 core-01 docker[830]: Hello World
May 26 22:05:56 core-01 docker[830]: Hello World
May 26 22:05:57 core-01 docker[830]: Hello World
May 26 22:05:58 core-01 docker[830]: Hello World
May 26 22:05:59 core-01 docker[830]: Hello World
May 26 22:06:00 core-01 docker[830]: Hello World
```

2. Stopping the service:

   `$ sudo systemctl stop hello.service`

3. You might need to kill the service, but that will not stop the `docker` container:

   `$ sudo systemctl kill hello.service`

   `$ docker ps`

   You should see a similar output as follows:

```
CONTAINER ID        IMAGE               COMMAND                  CREATED
    STATUS              PORTS               NAMES
aaadf696eb50        busybox:latest      "/bin/sh -c 'while t   13 seconds ago
    Up 13 seconds                           busybox1
```

4. As you can see, the `docker` container is still running. Hence, we need to stop it with the following command:

   `$ docker stop busybox1`

5. Restarting the service:

```
$ sudo systemctl restart hello.service
```

6. If you have changed `hello.service`, then before restarting, you need to reload all the service files:

```
$ sudo systemctl daemon-reload
```

7. Disabling the service:

```
$ sudo systemctl disable hello.service
```

The `systemd` service units can only run and be controlled on a single machine, and they should better be used for simpler tasks, for example, to download some files on reboot and so on.

You will continue learning about `systemd` in the next topic and in later chapters.

Getting started with fleet

We use `fleet` to take advantage of `systemd` at the higher level. The `fleet` is a cluster manager that controls `systemd` at the cluster level. You can even use it on a single machine and get all the advantages of `fleet` there too.

It encourages users to write applications as small, ephemeral units that can be easily migrated around a cluster of self-updating CoreOS machines.

The fleet unit files

The `fleet` unit files are regular `systemd` units combined with specific `fleet` properties.

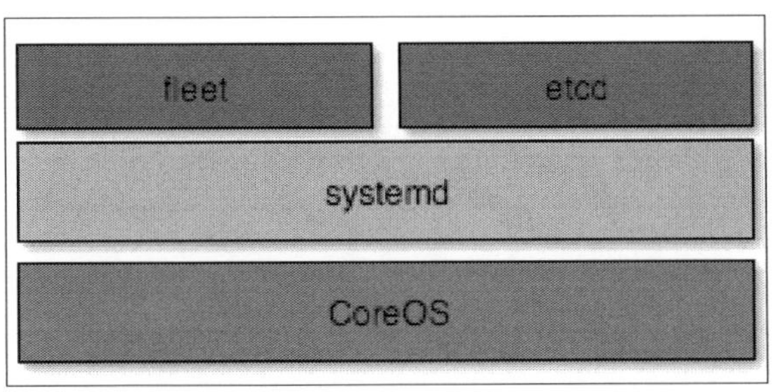

They are the primary interaction with `fleet`. As in the `systemd` units, the `fleet` units define what you want to do and how `fleet` should do it. The `fleet` will schedule a valid unit file to the single machine or a machine in a cluster, taking in mind the `fleet` special properties from the `[X-Fleet]` section, which replaces the `systemd` unit's `[Install]` section. The rest of `systemd` sections are same in `fleet` units.

Let's overview the specific options of `fleet` for the `[X-Fleet]` section:

- `MachineID`: This unit will be scheduled on the machine identified by a given string.
- `MachineOf`: This limits eligible machines to the one that hosts a specific unit.
- `MachineMetadata`: This limits eligible machines to those hosts with this specific metadata.
- `Conflicts`: This prevents a unit from being collocated with other units using glob-matching on other unit names.
- `Global`: Schedule this unit on all machines in the cluster. A unit is considered invalid if options other than MachineMetadata are provided alongside `Global=true`.

An example of how a `fleet` unit file can be written with the [X-Fleet] section is as follows:

```
[Unit]
Description=Ping google

[Service]
ExecStart=/usr/bin/ping google.com

[X-Fleet]
MachineMetadata=role=check
Conflicts=ping.*
```

So, let's see how `Conflicts=ping*` works. For instance, we have two identical `ping.1.service` and `ping.2.service` files, and we run on our cluster using the following code:

```
fleetctl start ping.*
```

This will schedule two `fleet` units on two separate cluster machines. So, let's convert the `systemd` unit called `hello.service` that we previously used to `fleet` unit.

1. As usual, you need to log in to the host via `ssh` with `vagrant ssh`.
2. Now let's create a simple unit file with the new name `hello1.service`:

   ```
   $ sudo vi hello1.service
   ```

   Press *I* and copy and paste the text as follows:

   ```
   [Unit]
   Description=HelloWorld
   # this unit will only start after docker.service
   ```

```
After=docker.service
Requires=docker.service

[Service]
TimeoutStartSec=0
# busybox image will be pulled from docker public registry
ExecStartPre=/usr/bin/docker pull busybox
# we use rm just in case the container with the name "busybox2" is
left
ExecStartPre=-/usr/bin/docker rm busybox2
# we start docker container
ExecStart=/usr/bin/docker run --rm --name busybox2 busybox /bin/sh
-c "while true; do echo Hello World; sleep 1; done"
# we stop docker container when systemctl stop is used
ExecStop=/usr/bin/docker stop busybox1

[X-Fleet]
```

3. Press *Esc* and then type `:wq` to save the file.

   As you can see, we have the `[X-Fleet]` section empty for now because we have nothing to use there yet. We will cover that part in more detail in the upcoming chapters.

4. First, we need to submit our `fleet` unit :

   `$ fleetctl submit hello1.service`

5. Let's verify that our `fleet` unit files:

   `$ fleetctl list-unit-files`

```
UNIT            HASH     DSTATE     STATE      TARGET
hello1.service  b5ef016  inactive   inactive   -
```

6. To start the new unit, run this command:

   `$ fleetctl start hello1.service`

```
Unit hello1.service launched on 4f17419c.../172.17.8.101
```

The preceding commands have submitted and started `hello1.service`.

Let's verify that our new `fleet` unit is running:

```
$ fleetctl list-units
```

Okay, it's now time to overview the `fleetctl` commands.

An overview of fleetctl

The `fleetctl` commands are very similar to `systemctl` commands— you can see this as follows—and we do not have to use `sudo` with `fleetctl`. Here are some tasks you can perform, listed with the required commands:

1. Checking the status of the unit:

   ```
   $ fleetctl status hello1.service
   ```

2. Stopping the service:

   ```
   $ fleetctl stop hello1.service
   ```

3. Viewing the service file:

   ```
   $ fleetctl cat hello1.service
   ```

4. If you want to just upload the unit file:

   ```
   $ fleetctl submit hello1.service
   ```

5. Listing all running fleet units:

   ```
   $ fleetctl list-units
   ```

6. Listing fleet cluster machines:

   ```
   $ fleetctl list-machines
   ```

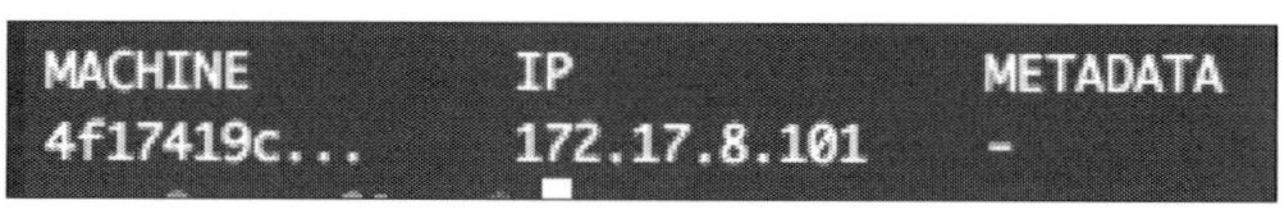

We see just one machine, as in our case, as we have only one machine running there.

Of course, if we want to see the `hello1.service` log output, we still use the same systemd `journalctl` command, as follows:

```
$ journalctl -f -u hello1.service
```

You should see the unit's output similar to this:

```
-- Logs begin at Thu 2015-05-14 21:52:42 . --
May 26 23:26:51 core-01 docker[6536]: Hello World
May 26 23:26:52 core-01 docker[6536]: Hello World
May 26 23:26:53 core-01 docker[6536]: Hello World
May 26 23:26:54 core-01 docker[6536]: Hello World
May 26 23:26:55 core-01 docker[6536]: Hello World
May 26 23:26:56 core-01 docker[6536]: Hello World
May 26 23:26:57 core-01 docker[6536]: Hello World
```

References

You can read more about these topics at the given URLs:

- **systemd unit files**: `https://coreos.com/docs/launching-containers/launching/getting-started-with-systemd/`
- **fleet unit files**: `https://coreos.com/docs/launching-containers/launching/fleet-unit-files/`

Summary

In this chapter, you learned about CoreOS's `systemd` init system. You also learned how to create and control system and `fleet` service units with `systemctl` and `fleetctl`.

In the next chapter, you will learn how to set up and manage CoreOS clusters.

4
Managing Clusters

In this chapter, we will cover how to setup and manage a local CoreOS cluster on a personal computer. You will learn how to bootstrap a three-peer cluster, customize it via the `cloud-config` file, and schedule a fleet unit in the cluster.

In this chapter, we will cover the following topics:

- Bootstrapping a local cluster
- Customizing a cluster via the`cloud-config` file
- Scheduling a `fleet` unit in the cluster

You are going to learn how to setup a simple three-node cluster on your personal computer.

Determining the optimal etcd cluster size

The most efficient cluster size is between three and nine peers. For larger clusters, `etcd` will select a subset of instances to participate in order to keep it efficient.

The bigger the cluster, the slower the writing to the cluster becomes, as all of the data needs to be replicated around the cluster peers. To have a cluster well-optimized, it needs to be based on an odd number of peers. It must have a quorum of at least of three peers and prevent a split-brain in the event of network partition.

In our case, we are going to set up a three-peer `etcd` cluster. To build a highly available cluster on the cloud (GCE, AWS, Azure, and so on), you should use multiple availability zones in order to decrease the effect of failure in a single domain.

In a general cluster, peers are not recommended to be used for anything except for running an `etcd` cluster. But for testing our cluster setup, it will be fine to deploy some `fleet` units there.

In later chapters, you will learn how to properly set up clusters to be used for production.

Bootstrapping a local cluster

As discussed earlier, we will be installing a three-peer `etcd` cluster on our computer.

Cloning the coreos-vagrant project

Let's clone the project and get it running. Follow these steps:

1. In your terminal or command prompt, type this:

   ```
   $ mkdir cluster
   $ cd cluster
   $ git clone https://github.com/coreos/coreos-vagrant.git
   $ cd coreos-vagrant
   $ cpconfig.rb.sampleconfig.rb
   $ cp user-data.sample user-data
   ```

2. Now we need to adjust some settings. Edit `config.rb` and change the file's top part to this example:

   ```
   # Size of the CoreOS cluster created by Vagrant
   $num_instances=3

   # Used to fetch a new discovery token for a cluster of size $num_
   instances
   $new_discovery_url="https://discovery.etcd.io/new?size=#{$num_
   instances}"

   # To automatically replace the discovery token on 'vagrant up',
   uncomment
   # the lines below:
   #
   if File.exists?('user-data') &&ARGV[0].eql?('up')
     require 'open-uri'
     require 'yaml'
   ```

```
    token = open($new_discovery_url).read

    data = YAML.load(IO.readlines('user-data')[1..-1].join)
    if data['coreos'].key? 'etcd'
      data['coreos']['etcd']['discovery'] = token
    end
    if data['coreos'].key? 'etcd2'
      data['coreos']['etcd2']['discovery'] = token
    end

  yaml = YAML.dump(data)
  File.open('user-data', 'w') { |file| file.write("#cloud-config\n\
  n#{yaml}") }
  end
  #
```

> Alternatively, you can use the example code of this chapter, which will be kept up to date with changes in the coreos-vagrant GitHub repository.

What we did here is as follows:

- We set the cluster to three instances
- Discovery token is automatically replaced on each vagrant up command

3. Next, we need to edit the user data file:

   Change the "#discovery: https://discovery.etcd.io/<token>" line to this:

   "discovery: https://discovery.etcd.io/<token>"

   So, when we boot our vagrant-based cluster the next time, we will have three CoreOS etcd peers running and connected to the same cluster via the discovery token provided through "https://discovery.etcd.io/<token>".

4. Let's now fire up our new cluster using the following command:

```
$ vagrant up
```

We should see something like this in our terminal:

```
Bringing machine 'core-01' up with 'virtualbox' provider...
Bringing machine 'core-02' up with 'virtualbox' provider...
Bringing machine 'core-03' up with 'virtualbox' provider...
==> core-01: Importing base box 'coreos-alpha'...
==> core-01: Matching MAC address for NAT networking...
==> core-01: Checking if box 'coreos-alpha' is up to date...
==> core-01: Setting the name of the VM: coreos-vagrant_core-01_1432759615645_90617
==> core-01: Clearing any previously set network interfaces...
==> core-01: Preparing network interfaces based on configuration...
    core-01: Adapter 1: nat
    core-01: Adapter 2: hostonly
==> core-01: Forwarding ports...
    core-01: 22 => 2222 (adapter 1)
==> core-01: Running 'pre-boot' VM customizations...
==> core-01: Booting VM...
==> core-01: Waiting for machine to boot. This may take a few minutes...
    core-01: SSH address: 127.0.0.1:2222
    core-01: SSH username: core
    core-01: SSH auth method: private key
    core-01: Warning: Connection timeout. Retrying...
==> core-01: Machine booted and ready!
==> core-01: Setting hostname...
==> core-01: Configuring and enabling network interfaces...
```

Hold on! There's more output!

```
    core-02: Running: inline script
==> core-03: Importing base box 'coreos-alpha'...
==> core-03: Matching MAC address for NAT networking...
==> core-03: Checking if box 'coreos-alpha' is up to date...
==> core-03: Setting the name of the VM: coreos-vagrant_core-03_1432759657821_10421
==> core-03: Fixed port collision for 22 => 2222. Now on port 2201.
==> core-03: Clearing any previously set network interfaces...
==> core-03: Preparing network interfaces based on configuration...
    core-03: Adapter 1: nat
    core-03: Adapter 2: hostonly
==> core-03: Forwarding ports...
    core-03: 22 => 2201 (adapter 1)
==> core-03: Running 'pre-boot' VM customizations...
==> core-03: Booting VM...
==> core-03: Waiting for machine to boot. This may take a few minutes...
    core-03: SSH address: 127.0.0.1:2201
    core-03: SSH username: core
    core-03: SSH auth method: private key
    core-03: Warning: Connection timeout. Retrying...
==> core-03: Machine booted and ready!
==> core-03: Setting hostname...
==> core-03: Configuring and enabling network interfaces...
==> core-03: Running provisioner: file...
==> core-03: Running provisioner: shell...
    core-03: Running: inline script
```

The cluster should be up and running now.

5. To check the status of the cluster, type the following command:

   $ vagrant status

   You should see something like what is shown in the following screenshot:

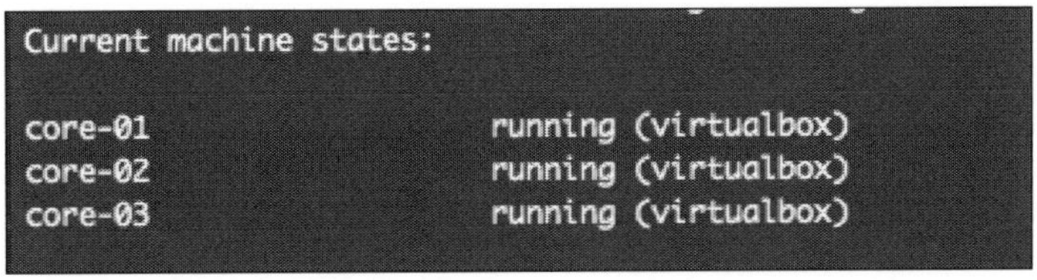

Now it's time to test our new CoreOS cluster. We need to run `ssh` for one of our peers and check the `fleet` machines. This can be done by the following command:

$ vagrant ssh core-01 -- -A

$ fleetctl list-machines

We should see something like what is shown in the following screenshot:

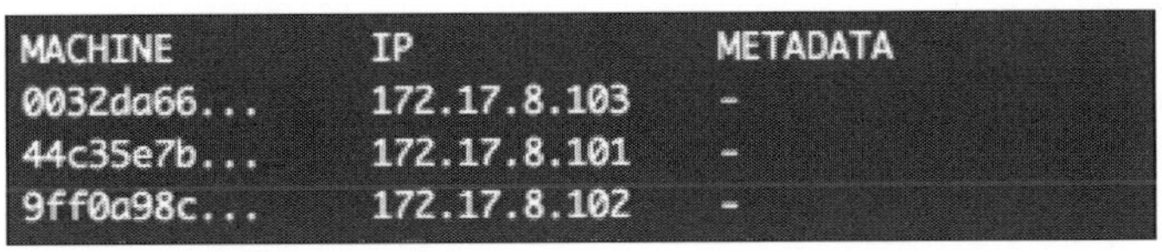

Excellent! We have got our first CoreOS cluster set, as we see all the three machines up and running. Now, let's try to set a key in `etcd` with which we can check on another machine later on. Type in the following command:

$ etcdctl set etcd-cluster-key "Hello CoreOS"

You will see the following output:

Hello CoreOS

Press *Ctrl+D* to exit and type the following command to get to VM host's console:

$ vagrant ssh core-02 -- -A

Let's verify that we can see our new `etcd` key there too:

$ etcdctl get etcd-cluster-key

Hello CoreOS

Brilliant! Our `etcd` cluster is working just fine.

Exit from the `core-02` machine by pressing *Ctrl+D*.

Customizing a cluster via the cloud-config file

Let's make some changes to the `cloud-config` file and push it into the cluster machines:

1. In the user data file (`cloud-config` file for Vagrant-based CoreOS), below the text block `fleet` make changes:

   ```
   public-ip: $public_ipv4
   ```

   Add a new line:

   ```
   metadata: cluster=vagrant
   ```

   So, it will look like this:

   ```
   fleet:
         public-ip: $public_ipv4
         metadata: cluster=vagrant
   ```

2. Let's add a `test.txt` file to the `/home/core` folder via `cloud-config` too. At the end of the user data file, add this code:

   ```
   write_files:
     - path: /home/core/test.txt
       permissions: 0644
       owner: core
       content: |
   Hello Cluster
   ```

   This will add a new file in the`/home/core` folder on each cluster machine.

3. To get our changes implemented which we did previously, run the following commands:

   ```
   $ vagrant provision
   ```

   You will see the following result:

   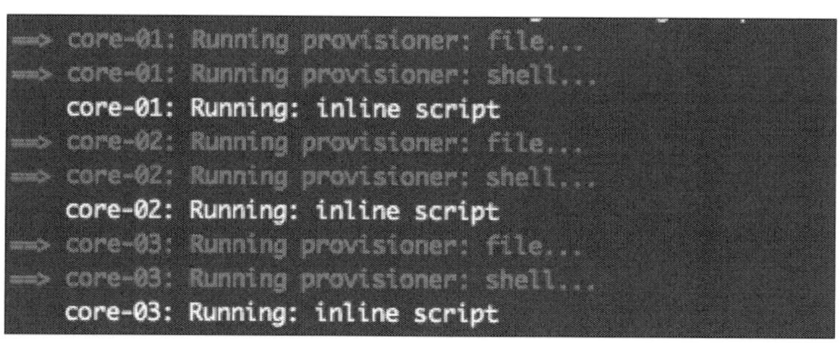

   Then, run this command:

   ```
   $ vagrant reload
   ```

The first command provisionally updated user data file on all three VMs, and the second reloaded them.

4. To `ssh` to one of the VMs, enter this code:

```
$ vagrant ssh core-03 -- -A
$ ls
test.txt
```

5. To check the content of the `test.txt` file, use this line:

```
$ cat test.txt
```

You should see output as follows:

```
Hello Cluster
```

As you can see, we have added some files to all cluster machines via the `cloud-config` file.

Let's check one more change that we have done in that file using the following command:

```
$ fleetctl list-machines
```

You will see something like this:

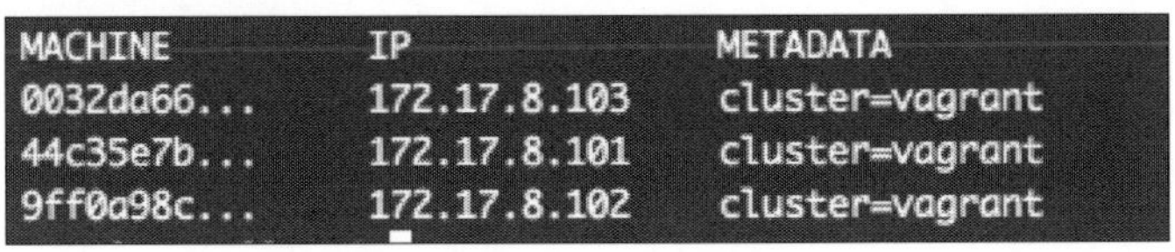

Thus, you can see that we have some metadata assigned to cluster machines via the `cloud-init` file.

Scheduling a fleet unit in the cluster

Now, for the fun part, we will schedule a `fleet` unit in the cluster.

1. Let's log in to the `core-03` machine:

```
$ vagrant ssh core-03 -- -A
```

2. Create a new `fleet` unit called `hello-cluster.service` by copying and pasting this line:

```
$ vi hello-cluster.service
[Unit]
[Service]
ExecStart=/usr/bin/bash -c "while true; do echo 'Hello
Cluster'; sleep 1; done"
```

3. Let's schedule the `hello-cluster.service` job for the cluster:

   ```
   $ fleetctl start hello-cluster.service
   ```

   You should see output as follows:

   ```
   Unit hello-cluster.service launched on
   bb53c039.../172.17.8.103
   ```

   We can see that `hello-cluster.service` was scheduled to be run on the `172.17.8.103` machine because that machine first responded to the `fleetctl` command.

   In later chapters, you will learn how to specifically schedule jobs to a particular machine. Now let's check out the real-time `hello-cluster.service` log:

   ```
   $ journalctl -u hello-cluster.service-f
   ```

   You will see something like this:

   ```
   -- Logs begin at Wed 2015-05-27 20:47:44 . --
   May 27 21:27:17 core-03 bash[790]: Hello Cluster
   May 27 21:27:18 core-03 bash[790]: Hello Cluster
   May 27 21:27:19 core-03 bash[790]: Hello Cluster
   May 27 21:27:20 core-03 bash[790]: Hello Cluster
   May 27 21:27:21 core-03 bash[790]: Hello Cluster
   May 27 21:27:22 core-03 bash[790]: Hello Cluster
   May 27 21:27:23 core-03 bash[790]: Hello Cluster
   May 27 21:27:24 core-03 bash[790]: Hello Cluster
   ```

4. To exit from the VM and reload the cluster, type the following command:

   ```
   $ vagrant reload
   ```

5. Now, `ssh` again back to any machine:

   ```
   $ vagrant ssh core-02 -- -A
   ```

6. Then run this command:

   ```
   $ fleetctl list-units
   ```

   The following output will be seen:

   ```
   UNIT                   MACHINE                    ACTIVE  SUB
   hello-cluster.service  44c35e7b.../172.17.8.101   active  running
   ```

7. As you can see, `hello-cluster.service` got scheduled on another machine; in our case, it is `core-01`. Suppose we `ssh` to it:

   $ vagrant ssh core-01 -- -A

8. Then, we run the following command there. As a result, we will see the real-time log again:

   $ journalctl -u hello-cluster.service-f

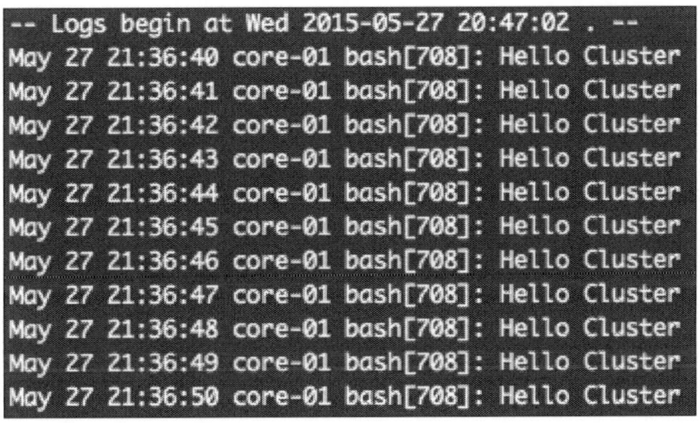

```
-- Logs begin at Wed 2015-05-27 20:47:02 . --
May 27 21:36:40 core-01 bash[708]: Hello Cluster
May 27 21:36:41 core-01 bash[708]: Hello Cluster
May 27 21:36:42 core-01 bash[708]: Hello Cluster
May 27 21:36:43 core-01 bash[708]: Hello Cluster
May 27 21:36:44 core-01 bash[708]: Hello Cluster
May 27 21:36:45 core-01 bash[708]: Hello Cluster
May 27 21:36:46 core-01 bash[708]: Hello Cluster
May 27 21:36:47 core-01 bash[708]: Hello Cluster
May 27 21:36:48 core-01 bash[708]: Hello Cluster
May 27 21:36:49 core-01 bash[708]: Hello Cluster
May 27 21:36:50 core-01 bash[708]: Hello Cluster
```

References

You can read more about how to use cloud-config at `https://coreos.com/docs/cluster-management/setup/cloudinit-cloud-config/`.You can find out more about Vagrant at `https://docs.vagrantup.com`.If you have any issues or questions about Vagrant, you can subscribe to the Vagrant Google group at `https://groups.google.com/forum/#!forum/vagrant-up`.

Summary

In this chapter,you learned how to set up aCoreOS cluster, customize it via cloud-config, schedule `fleet` service units to the cluster, and check the `fleet` unit in the cluster status and log.In the next chapter,you will learn how to perform local and cloud development setups.

5
Building a Development Environment

In this chapter, we will cover how to set up a local CoreOS environment for development on a personal computer, and a test and staging environment cluster on the VM instances of Google Cloud's Compute Engine. These are the topics we will cover:

- Setting up a local development environment
- Bootstrapping a remote test/staging cluster on GCE

Setting up the local development environment

We are going to learn how to set up a development environment on our personal computer with the help of VirtualBox and Vagrant, as we did in an earlier chapter. Building and testing `docker` images and coding locally makes you more productive, it saves time, and Docker repository can be pushed to the docker registry (private or not) when your docker images are ready. The same goes for the code; you just work on it and test it locally. When it is ready, you can merge it with the git test branch where your team/client can test it further.

Setting up the development VM

In the previous chapters, you learned how to install CoreOS via Vagrant on your PC. Here, we have prepared installation scripts for Linux and OS X to go straight to the point. You can download the latest *CoreOS Essentials* book example files from GitHub repository:

```
$ git clone https://github.com/rimusz/coreos-essentials-book/
```

To install a local Vagrant-based development VM, type this:

```
$ cd coreos-essentials-book/chapter5/Local_Development_VM
$ ./install_local_dev.sh
```

You should see an output similar to this:

```
Setting up CoreOS VM
==> core-dev-01: Checking for updates to 'coreos-alpha'
    core-dev-01: Latest installed version: 695.0.0
    core-dev-01: Version constraints: >= 308.0.1
    core-dev-01: Provider: virtualbox
==> core-dev-01: Box 'coreos-alpha' (v695.0.0) is running the latest version.
Bringing machine 'core-dev-01' up with 'virtualbox' provider...
==> core-dev-01: Importing base box 'coreos-alpha'...
==> core-dev-01: Matching MAC address for NAT networking...
==> core-dev-01: Checking if box 'coreos-alpha' is up to date...
==> core-dev-01: Setting the name of the VM: vm_core-dev-01_1433075600788_15889
==> core-dev-01: Clearing any previously set network interfaces...
==> core-dev-01: Preparing network interfaces based on configuration...
    core-dev-01: Adapter 1: nat
    core-dev-01: Adapter 2: hostonly
==> core-dev-01: Forwarding ports...
    core-dev-01: 2375 => 2375 (adapter 1)
    core-dev-01: 22 => 2222 (adapter 1)
==> core-dev-01: Running 'pre-boot' VM customizations...
==> core-dev-01: Booting VM...
==> core-dev-01: Waiting for machine to boot. This may take a few minutes...
    core-dev-01: SSH address: 127.0.0.1:2222
    core-dev-01: SSH username: core
    core-dev-01: SSH auth method: private key
    core-dev-01: Warning: Connection timeout. Retrying...
==> core-dev-01: Machine booted and ready!
==> core-dev-01: Setting hostname...
==> core-dev-01: Configuring and enabling network interfaces...
==> core-dev-01: Exporting NFS shared folders...
==> core-dev-01: Preparing to edit /etc/exports. Administrator privileges will be required...
==> core-dev-01: Mounting NFS shared folders...
==> core-dev-01: Running provisioner: file...
==> core-dev-01: Running provisioner: shell...
    core-dev-01: Running: inline script
```

Hang on! There's more!

```
Connection to 127.0.0.1 closed.
Downloading etcdctl 2.0.11 for OS X
  % Total    % Received % Xferd  Average Speed   Time    Time     Time  Current
                                 Dload  Upload   Total   Spent    Left  Speed
100   407    0   407    0     0    190      0 --:--:--  0:00:02 --:--:--   190
100 5042k  100 5042k    0     0   908k      0  0:00:05  0:00:05 --:--:-- 1602k
Archive:  etcd.zip
  inflating: etcdctl
Connection to 127.0.0.1 closed.
Downloading fleetctl v0.10.1 for OS X
  % Total    % Received % Xferd  Average Speed   Time    Time     Time  Current
                                 Dload  Upload   Total   Spent    Left  Speed
100   410    0   410    0     0    638      0 --:--:-- --:--:-- --:--:--   638
100 2483k  100 2483k    0     0   893k      0  0:00:02  0:00:02 --:--:-- 1540k
Archive:  fleet.zip
  inflating: fleetctl
Connection to 127.0.0.1 closed.
Downloading docker v1.6.2 client for OS X
  % Total    % Received % Xferd  Average Speed   Time    Time     Time  Current
                                 Dload  Upload   Total   Spent    Left  Speed
100 7299k  100 7299k    0     0  1262k      0  0:00:05  0:00:05 --:--:-- 1714k
Installation has finished !!!

Press [Enter] key to continue...
```

This will perform a VM installation similar to the installation that we did in *Chapter 1, CoreOS – Overview and Installation,* but in a more automated way this time.

What happened during the VM installation?

Let's check out what happened during the VM installation. To sum up:

- A new CoreOS VM (VirtualBox/Vagrant-based) was installed
- A new folder called `coreos-dev-env` was created in your `Home` folder

Run the following commands:

```
$ cd ~/coreos-dev-env
$ ls
bin
fleet
share
vm
vm_halt.sh
vm_ssh.sh
vm_up.sh
```

As a result, this is what we see:

- Four folders, which consist of the following list:
    - `bin`: `docker`, `etcdctl` and `fleetctl` files
    - `fleet`: The `nginx.service fleet` unit is stored here
    - `share`: This is shared folder between the host and VM
    - `vm`: Vagrantfile, `config.rb` and `user-data` files
- We also have three files:
    - `vm_halt.sh`: This is used to shut down the CoreOS VM
    - `vm_ssh.sh`: This is used to `ssh` to the CoreOS VM
    - `vm_up.sh`: This is used to start the CoreOS VM, with the OS shell preset to the following:

```
# Set the environment variable for the docker daemon
export DOCKER_HOST=tcp://127.0.0.1:2375
# path to the bin folder where we store our binary files
export PATH=${HOME}/coreos-dev-env/bin:$PATH
# set etcd endpoint
export ETCDCTL_PEERS=http://172.19.20.99:2379
# set fleetctl endpoint
export FLEETCTL_ENDPOINT=http://172.19.20.99:2379
export FLEETCTL_DRIVER=etcd
export FLEETCTL_STRICT_HOST_KEY_CHECKING=false
```

Now that we have installed our CoreOS VM, let's run `vm_up.sh`. We should see this output in the **Terminal** window:

```
$ cd ~/coreos-dev-env
$ ./vm_up.sh
```

You should see output similar to this:

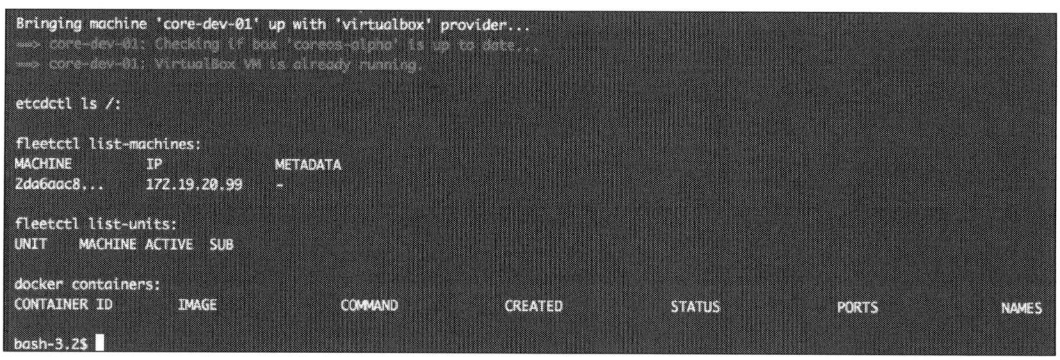

As we can see in the preceding screenshot, we do not have any errors. Only `fleetctl list-machines` shows our CoreOS VM machine, and we have no `docker` containers and `fleet` units running there yet.

Deploying the fleet units

Let's deploy some fleet units to verify that our development environment works fine. Run the following commands:

```
$ cd fleet
$ fleetctl start nginx.service
```

> It can take a bit of time for docker to download the `nginx` image.

You can check out the `nginx.service` unit's status:

```
$ fleetctl status nginx.service
```

You should see output similar to this:

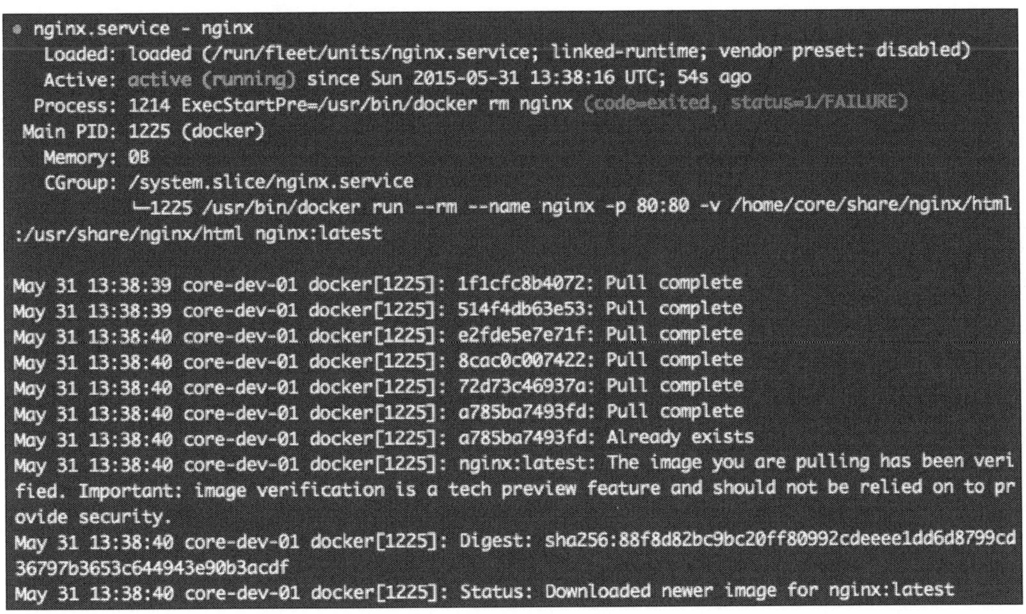

Once the `nginx fleet` unit is deployed, open in your browser `http://172.19.20.99`. You should see the following message:

Let's check out what happened there. We scheduled this `nginx.service` unit with `fleetctl`:

```
$ cat ~/coreos-dev-env/fleet/nginx.service
```

```
[Unit]
Description=nginx

[Service]
User=core
TimeoutStartSec=0
EnvironmentFile=/etc/environment
ExecStartPre=-/usr/bin/docker rm nginx
ExecStart=/usr/bin/docker run --rm --name nginx -p 80:80 \
 -v /home/core/share/nginx/html:/usr/share/nginx/html \
 nginx:latest
#
ExecStop=/usr/bin/docker stop nginx
ExecStopPost=-/usr/bin/docker rm nginx

Restart=always
RestartSec=10s

[X-Fleet]
```

Then, we used the official `nginx` image from the docker registry, and shared our local `~/coreos-dev-env/share` folder with `/home/core/share`, which was mounted afterwards as a docker volume `/home/core/share/nginx/html:/usr/share/nginx/html`.

So, whatever `html` files we put into our local `~/coreos-dev-env/share/nginx/html` folder will be picked up automatically by `nginx`.

Let's overview what advantages such a setup gives us:

- We can build and test docker containers locally, and then push them to the docker registry (private or public).
- Test our code locally and push it to the git repository when we are done with it.
- By having a local development setup, productivity really increases, as everything is done much faster. We do not have build new docker containers upon every code change, push them to the remote docker registry, pull them at some remote test servers, and so on.
- It is very easy to clean up the setup and get it working from a clean start again, reusing the configured `fleet` units to start the all required docker containers.

Very good! So, now, we have a fully operational local development setup!

> This setup is as per the CoreOS documentation at `https://coreos.com/docs/cluster-management/setup/cluster-architectures/`, in the *Docker Dev Environment on Laptop* section.
>
> Go through the `coreos-dev-install.sh` bash script, which sets up your local development VM. It is a simple script and is well commented, so it should not be too hard to understand its logic.

If you are a Mac user, you can download from `https://github.com/rimusz/coreos-osx-gui` and use my Mac App **CoreOS-Vagrant GUI for Mac OS X**, which has a nice UI to manage CoreOS VM. It will automatically set up the CoreOS VM environment.

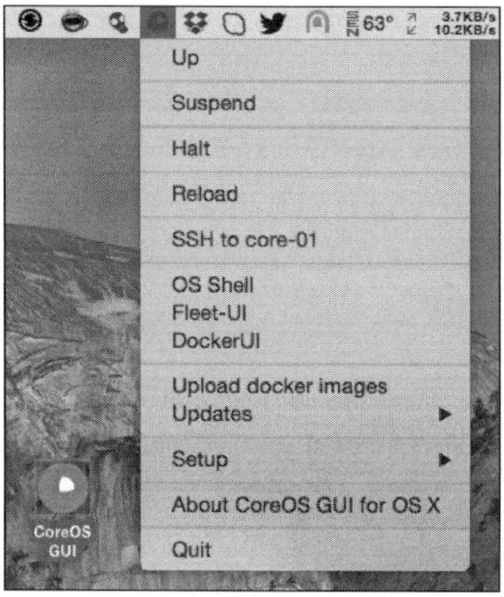

Bootstrapping a remote test/staging cluster on GCE

So, we have successfully built our local development setup. Let's get to the next level, that is, building our test/staging environment on the cloud.

We are going to use Google Cloud's Compute Engine, so you need a Google Cloud account for this. If you do not have it, for the purpose of running the examples in the book, you can open a trial account at `https://cloud.google.com/compute/`. A trial account lasts for 60 days and has $300 as credits, enough to run all of this book's examples. When you are done with opening the account, Google Cloud SDK needs to be installed from `https://cloud.google.com/sdk/`.

In this topic, we will follow the recommendations on how to set up CoreOS cluster by referring to *Easy Development/Testing Cluster* from `https://coreos.com/docs/cluster-management/setup/cluster-architectures/`.

Test/staging cluster setup

Okay, let's get our cloud cluster installed, as you have already downloaded this book's code examples. Carry out these steps in the shown order:

1. Run the following commands:

```
$ cd coreos-essentials-book/chapter5/Test_Staging_Cluster
$ ls
cloud-config
create_cluster_control.sh
create_cluster_workers.sh
files
fleet
install_fleetctl_and_scripts.sh
settings

Let's check "settings" file first:
$ cat settings
### CoreOS Test/Staging Cluster on GCE settings

## change Google Cloud settings as per your requirements
# GC settings

# CoreOS RELEASE CHANNEL
channel=beta

# SET YOUR PROJECT AND ZONE !!!
project=my-cloud-project
zone=europe-west1-d

# ETCD CONTROL AND NODES MACHINES TYPE
#
control_machine_type=g1-small
#
worker_machine_type=n1-standard-1
##

###
```

2. Update the `settings` with your Google Cloud project ID and zone where you want the CoreOS instances to be deployed:

```
# SET YOUR PROJECT AND ZONE !!!
project=my-cloud-project
zone=europe-west1-d
```

3. Next, let's install our control server, which is our `etcd` cluster node:

```
$ ./create_cluster_control.sh
```

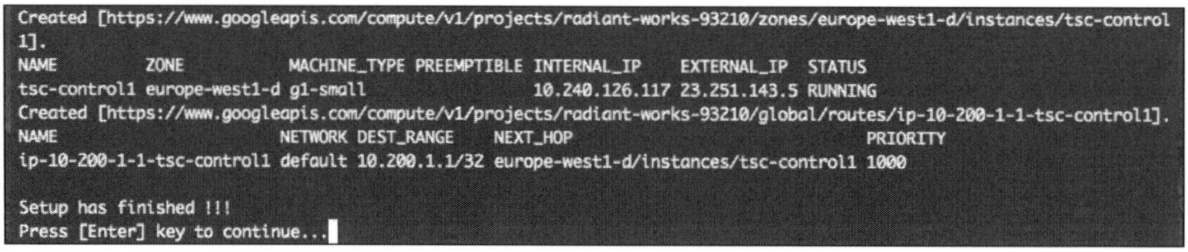

We just created our new cluster `etcd` control node.

1. Let's check out what we have in this script:

```
#!/bin/bash

# Create TS cluster control


# Update required settings in "settings" file before running this
script


function pause(){
read -p "$*"
}


## Fetch GC settings
# project and zone
project=$(cat settings | grep project= | head -1 | cut -f2 -d"=")
zone=$(cat settings | grep zone= | head -1 | cut -f2 -d"=")
# CoreOS release channel
channel=$(cat settings | grep channel= | head -1 | cut -f2 -d"=")
# control instance type
```

```
control_machine_type=$(cat settings | grep control_machine_type= |
head -1 | cut -f2 -d"=")

# get the latest full image name

image=$(gcloud compute images list --project=$project | grep -v
grep | grep coreos-$channel | awk {'print $1'})

##


# create an instance

gcloud compute instances create tsc-control1 --project=$project
--image=$image --image-project=coreos-cloud \

 --boot-disk-size=10 --zone=$zone --machine-type=$control_machine_
type \

 --metadata-from-file user-data=cloud-config/control1.yaml --can-
ip-forward --tags tsc-control1 tsc


# create a static IP for the new instance

gcloud compute routes create ip-10-200-1-1-tsc-control1
--project=$project \

 --next-hop-instance tsc-control1 \

 --next-hop-instance-zone $zone \

 --destination-range 10.200.1.1/32


echo " "

echo "Setup has finished !!!"

pause 'Press [Enter] key to continue...'

# end of bash script
```

It fetches the settings needed for Google Cloud from the `settings` file. With the help of `gcloud` utility from the Google Cloud SDK, it sets up the `tsld-control1` instance and assigns to it a static internal IP `10.200.1.1`. This IP will be used by workers to connect the `etcd` cluster, which will run on `tsc-control1`.

In the `cloud-config` folder, we have the `cloud-config` files needed to create CoreOS instances on GCE.

Open `control1.yaml` and check out what is there in it:

```
$ cat control1.yaml
#cloud-config

coreos:

etcd2:
    name: control1
    initial-advertise-peer-urls: http://10.200.1.1:2380
    initial-cluster-token: control_etcd
    initial-cluster: control1=http://10.200.1.1:2380
    initial-cluster-state: new
    listen-peer-urls: http://10.200.1.1:2380,http://10.200.1.1:7001
    listen-client-urls: http://0.0.0.0:2379,http://0.0.0.0:4001
    advertise-client-urls: http://10.200.1.1:2379,http://10.200.1.1:4001
  fleet:
    metadata: "role=services,cpeer=tsc-control1"
  units:
    - name: 00-ens4v1.network
      runtime: true
      content: |
        [Match]
        Name=ens4v1

        [Network]
        Address=10.200.1.1/24
    - name: etcd2.service
      command: start
    - name: fleet.service
      command: start
    - name: docker.service
      command: start
      drop-ins:
        - name: 50-insecure-registry.conf
          content: |
            [Unit]
            [Service]
```

```
            Environment=DOCKER_OPTS='--insecure-registry="0.0.0.0/0"'
write_files:
  - path: /etc/resolv.conf
    permissions: 0644
    owner: root
    content: |
      nameserver 169.254.169.254
      nameserver 10.240.0.1
#end of cloud-config
```

As you see, we have `cloud-config` file for the control machine, which does the following:

1. It creates a node `etcd` cluster with a static IP of `10.200.1.1`, which will be used to connect to `etcd` cluster.
2. It sets the `fleet` metadata to `role=services,cpeer=tsc-control1`.
3. `Unit 00-ens4v1.network` assigns a static IP of `10.200.1.1`.
4. The `docker.service` drop-in `50-insecure-registry.conf` sets `--insecure-registry="0.0.0.0/0"`, which allows you to connect to any privately hosted docker registry.
5. In the `write_files` part, we update `/etc/resolv.conf` with Google Cloud DNS servers, which sometimes do not get automatically put there if the static IP is assigned to the instance.

Creating our cluster workers

In order to create the cluster workers, the command to be used is as follows:

```
$ ./create_cluster_workers.sh
```

```
Created [https://www.googleapis.com/compute/v1/projects/radiant-works-93210/zones/europe-west1-d/inst
ances/tsc-test1].
NAME      ZONE           MACHINE_TYPE  PREEMPTIBLE INTERNAL_IP    EXTERNAL_IP  STATUS
tsc-test1 europe-west1-d n1-standard-1             10.240.129.115 23.251.143.5 RUNNING
Created [https://www.googleapis.com/compute/v1/projects/radiant-works-93210/zones/europe-west1-d/inst
ances/tsc-staging1].
NAME         ZONE           MACHINE_TYPE  PREEMPTIBLE INTERNAL_IP   EXTERNAL_IP   STATUS
tsc-staging1 europe-west1-d n1-standard-1             10.240.22.204 104.155.23.81 RUNNING
Created [https://www.googleapis.com/compute/v1/projects/radiant-works-93210/global/firewalls/http-80]
.
NAME    NETWORK SRC_RANGES RULES  SRC_TAGS TARGET_TAGS
http-80 default 0.0.0.0/0  tcp:80          tsc-test1,tsc-staging1

Setup has finished !!!
Press [Enter] key to continue...
```

Make a note of the workers' external IPs, as shown in the previous screenshot; we will need them later.

Of course, you can always check them at the Google Developers Console too.

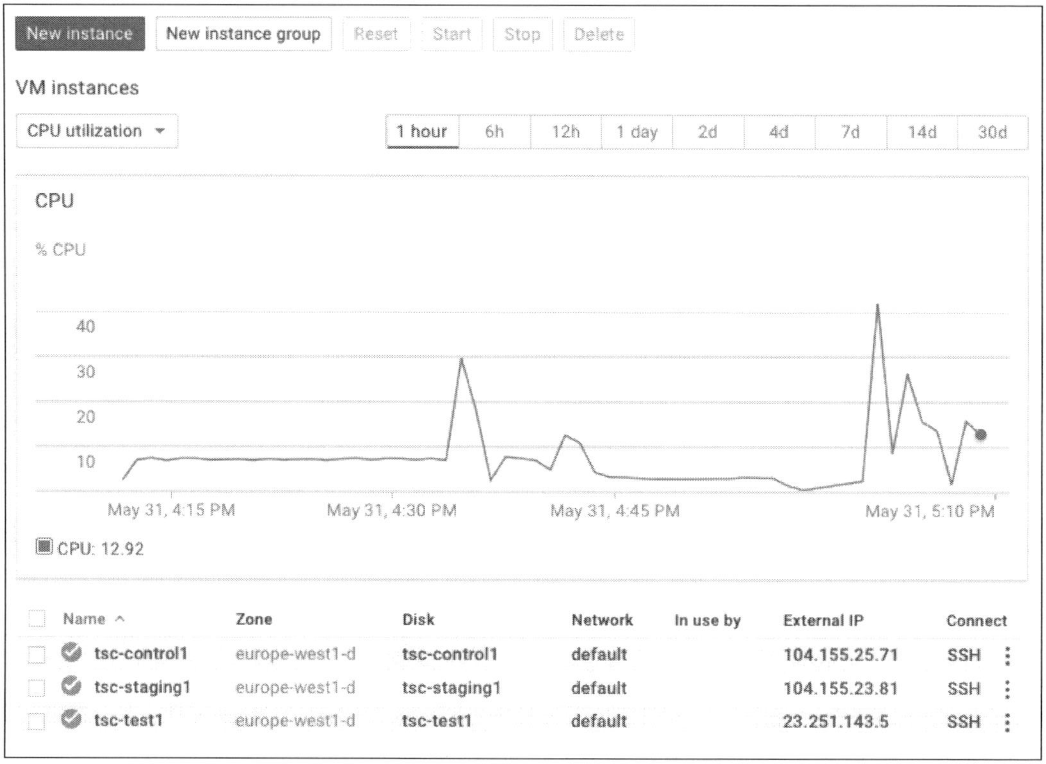

Let's check out what we have inside the `test1.yaml` and `staging1.yaml` files in the cloud-`config` folder. Run the following command:

```
$ cat test1.yaml
#cloud-config


coreos:
  etcd2:
    listen-client-urls: http://0.0.0.0:2379,http://0.0.0.0:4001
    initial-cluster: control1=http://10.200.1.1:2380
    proxy: on
  fleet:
    public-ip: $public_ipv4
```

```
    metadata: "role=worker,cpeer=tsc-test1"
  units:
    - name: etcd2.service
      command: start
    - name: fleet.service
      command: start
    - name: docker.service
      command: start
      drop-ins:
        - name: 50-insecure-registry.conf
          content: |
            [Unit]
            [Service]
            Environment=DOCKER_OPTS='--insecure-registry="0.0.0.0/0"'
# end of cloud-config
```

As we can see, we have `cloud-config` file for the `test1` machine:

- It connects to the `etcd` cluster machine `control1` and enables `etcd2` in proxy mode, which allows anything running on the host to access the `etcd` cluster via the `127.0.0.1` address
- It sets the `fleet` metadata `role=services,cpeer=tsc-test1`
- The `docker.service` drop-in `50-insecure-registry.conf` sets `--insecure-registry="0.0.0.0/0"`, which will allow you to connect to any privately hosted docker registry

That's it!

If you check out the `tsc-staging1.yaml` cloud-config file, you will see that it is almost identical to `test1.yaml`, except that the `fleet` metadata has `cpeer=tsc-staging1` in it. But we are not done yet!

Let's now install the OS X/Linux clients, which will allow us to manage the cloud development cluster from our local computer.

Let's run this installation script:

```
$ ./install_fleetctl_and_scripts.sh
```

You should see the following output:

```
Fetching Google Cloud settings ...

Creating 'coreos-tsc-gce' folder and its subfolders ...

Installing Development cluster local files ...

Downloading and instaling fleetctl ...
Downloading fleetctl v0.10.1 for OS X
  % Total    % Received % Xferd  Average Speed   Time    Time     Time  Current
                                 Dload  Upload   Total   Spent    Left  Speed
100   408    0   408    0     0    609      0 --:--:-- --:--:-- --:--:--   610
100 2483k  100 2483k    0     0  1099k      0  0:00:02  0:00:02 --:--:-- 1672k
Archive:  fleet.zip
  inflating: fleetctl

Installation has finished !!!
Press [Enter] key to continue...
```

So, what has the last script done?

In your home folder, it created a new folder called `~/coreos-tsc-gce`, which has two folders:

- `bin`
  - `etcdctl`: This is the shell script used to access the `etcdctl` client on a remote cluster `control1` node
  - `fleetctl`: The local `fleetctl` client is used to control the remote cluster
  - `staging1.sh`: Make `ssh` connection to remote `staging1` worker
  - `test1.sh`: Make `ssh` connection to remote `test1` worker
  - `set_cluster_access.sh`: This sets up shell access to the remote cluster
- `fleet`
  - `test1_webserver.service`: Our `test1` server's `fleet` unit
  - `staging1_webserver.service`: Our `staging1` server's `fleet` unit

Now, let's take a look at `set_cluster_access.sh`:

```
$ cd ~/coreos-tsc-gce/bin
$ cat set_cluster_access.sh
#!/bin/bash

# Setup Client SSH Tunnels
ssh-add ~/.ssh/google_compute_engine &>/dev/null

# SET
# path to the cluster folder where we store our binary files
export PATH=${HOME}/coreos-tsc-gce/bin:$PATH
# fleet tunnel
export FLEETCTL_TUNNEL=104.155.61.42 # our control1 external IP
export FLEETCTL_STRICT_HOST_KEY_CHECKING=false

echo "etcd cluster:"
etcdctl --no-sync ls /

echo "list fleet units:"
fleetctl list-units

/bin/bash
```

This script is preset by `./install_fleetctl_and_scripts.sh` with the remote `control1` external IP, and allows us to issue remote `fleet` control commands:

```
$ ./set_cluster_access.sh
```

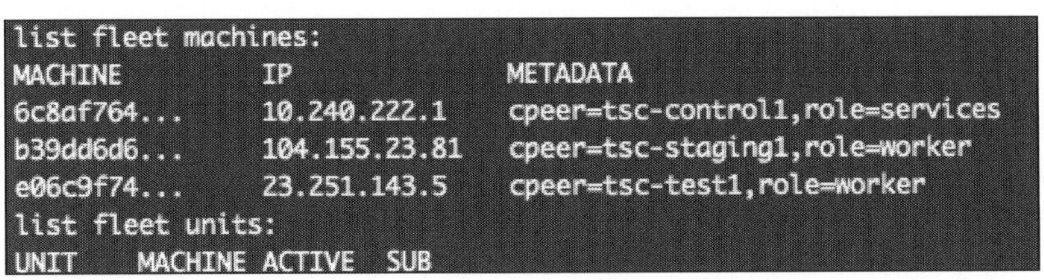

```
list fleet machines:
MACHINE         IP              METADATA
6c8af764...     10.240.222.1    cpeer=tsc-control1,role=services
b39dd6d6...     104.155.23.81   cpeer=tsc-staging1,role=worker
e06c9f74...     23.251.143.5    cpeer=tsc-test1,role=worker
list fleet units:
UNIT    MACHINE ACTIVE  SUB
```

Very good! Our cluster is up and running, and the workers are connected to the `etcd` cluster.

Now we can run `fleetctl` commands on the remote cluster from our local computer.

Running fleetctl commands on the remote cluster

Let's now install the `nginx` fleet units we have in the `~/coreos-tsc-gce/fleet` folder. Run the following command:

```
$ cd ~/coreos-tsc-gce/fleet
```

Let's first submit the `fleet` units to the cluster:

```
$ fleetctl submit *.service
```

Now, let's start them:

```
$ fleetctl start *.service
```

You should see something like what is shown in the following screenshot:

Give some time to docker to download the nginx image from the docker registry. We can then check the status of our newly deployed `fleet` units using the following command:

```
$ fleetctl status *.service
```

```
● staging1_webserver.service - nginx
   Loaded: loaded (/run/fleet/units/staging1_webserver.service; linked-runtime; vendor preset: disabled)
   Active: active (running) since Sun 2015-05-31 18:20:17 ; 1min 26s ago
  Process: 3276 ExecStartPre=/usr/bin/docker rm staging1-webserver (code=exited, status=1/FAILURE)
 Main PID: 3286 (docker)
   Memory: 2.5M
   CGroup: /system.slice/staging1_webserver.service
           └─3286 /usr/bin/docker run --rm --name staging1-webserver -p 80:80 -v /home/core/share/nginx/html:/usr/share/ng

May 31 18:20:31 tsc-staging1.c.radiant-works-93210.internal docker[3286]: 1f1cfc8b4072: Pull complete
May 31 18:20:31 tsc-staging1.c.radiant-works-93210.internal docker[3286]: 514f4db63e53: Pull complete
May 31 18:20:32 tsc-staging1.c.radiant-works-93210.internal docker[3286]: e2fde5e7e71f: Pull complete
May 31 18:20:32 tsc-staging1.c.radiant-works-93210.internal docker[3286]: 8cac0c007422: Pull complete
May 31 18:20:32 tsc-staging1.c.radiant-works-93210.internal docker[3286]: 72d73c46937a: Pull complete
May 31 18:20:33 tsc-staging1.c.radiant-works-93210.internal docker[3286]: a785ba7493fd: Pull complete
May 31 18:20:33 tsc-staging1.c.radiant-works-93210.internal docker[3286]: a785ba7493fd: Already exists
May 31 18:20:33 tsc-staging1.c.radiant-works-93210.internal docker[3286]: nginx:latest: The image you are pulling has been
ty.
May 31 18:20:33 tsc-staging1.c.radiant-works-93210.internal docker[3286]: Digest: sha256:88f8d82bc9bc20ff80992cdeeee1dd6d8
May 31 18:20:33 tsc-staging1.c.radiant-works-93210.internal docker[3286]: Status: Downloaded newer image for nginx:latest

● test1_webserver.service - nginx
   Loaded: loaded (/run/fleet/units/test1_webserver.service; linked-runtime; vendor preset: disabled)
   Active: active (running) since Sun 2015-05-31 18:20:17 ; 1min 27s ago
  Process: 2569 ExecStartPre=/usr/bin/docker rm test1-webserver (code=exited, status=1/FAILURE)
 Main PID: 2577 (docker)
   Memory: 2.5M
   CGroup: /system.slice/test1_webserver.service
           └─2577 /usr/bin/docker run --rm --name test1-webserver -p 80:80 -v /home/core/share/nginx/html:/usr/share/nginx

May 31 18:20:30 tsc-test1.c.radiant-works-93210.internal docker[2577]: 1f1cfc8b4072: Pull complete
May 31 18:20:30 tsc-test1.c.radiant-works-93210.internal docker[2577]: 514f4db63e53: Pull complete
May 31 18:20:31 tsc-test1.c.radiant-works-93210.internal docker[2577]: e2fde5e7e71f: Pull complete
May 31 18:20:32 tsc-test1.c.radiant-works-93210.internal docker[2577]: 8cac0c007422: Pull complete
May 31 18:20:32 tsc-test1.c.radiant-works-93210.internal docker[2577]: 72d73c46937a: Pull complete
May 31 18:20:33 tsc-test1.c.radiant-works-93210.internal docker[2577]: a785ba7493fd: Pull complete
May 31 18:20:33 tsc-test1.c.radiant-works-93210.internal docker[2577]: a785ba7493fd: Already exists
May 31 18:20:33 tsc-test1.c.radiant-works-93210.internal docker[2577]: nginx:latest: The image you are pulling has been ve
May 31 18:20:33 tsc-test1.c.radiant-works-93210.internal docker[2577]: Digest: sha256:88f8d82bc9bc20ff80992cdeeee1dd6d8799
May 31 18:20:33 tsc-test1.c.radiant-works-93210.internal docker[2577]: Status: Downloaded newer image for nginx:latest
```

Then, run this command:

```
$ fleetctl list-units
```

```
UNIT                          MACHINE                       ACTIVE   SUB
staging1_webserver.service    b39dd6d6.../104.155.23.81     active   running
test1_webserver.service       e06c9f74.../23.251.143.5      active   running
```

Perfect!

Now, in your web browser, open the workers' external IPs, and you should see this:

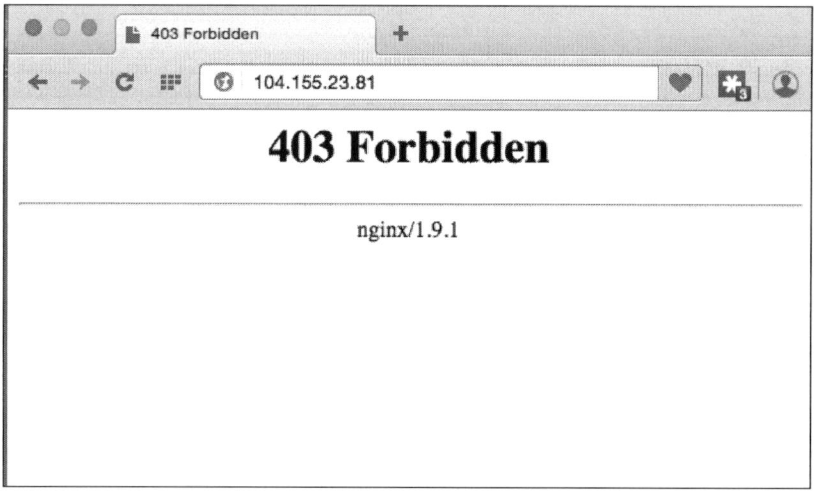

The `nginx` servers are now working. The reason they are showing this error message is that we have not provided any `index.html` file yet. We will do that in the next chapter.

But, before we finish this chapter, let's check out our `test/staging` `nginx` `fleet` units:

```
$ cd ~/coreos-tsc-gce/fleet
$ cat test1_webserver.service
```

You should see something like the following code:

```
[Unit]
Description=nginx

[Service]
User=core
TimeoutStartSec=0
EnvironmentFile=/etc/environment
ExecStartPre=-/usr/bin/docker rm nginx
ExecStart=/usr/bin/docker run --rm --name test1-webserver -p 80:80 \
-v /home/core/share/nginx/html:/usr/share/nginx/html \
nginx:latest
#
```

```
ExecStop=/usr/bin/docker stop nginx
ExecStopPost=-/usr/bin/docker rm nginx

Restart=always
RestartSec=10s
[X-Fleet]
MachineMetadata=cpeer=tsc-test1 # this where our fleet unit gets
scheduled
```

There are a few things to note here:

- `Staging1` has an almost identical unit; instead of `test1`, it has `staging1` there. So, we reused the same fleet unit as we used for our local development machine, with a few changes.
- At `ExecStart`, we used `test1-webserver` and `staging1-webserver`, so by using `fleetctl list-units`, we can see which one is which.

  We added this bit:

  ```
  [X-Fleet]
  MachineMetadata=cpeer=tsc-test1
  ```

This will schedule the unit to the particular cluster worker.

If you are a Mac user, you can download from `https://github.com/rimusz/coreos-osx-gui-cluster` and use my Mac App **CoreOS-Vagrant Cluster GUI for Mac OS X**, which has a nice UI for managing CoreOS VMs on your computer.

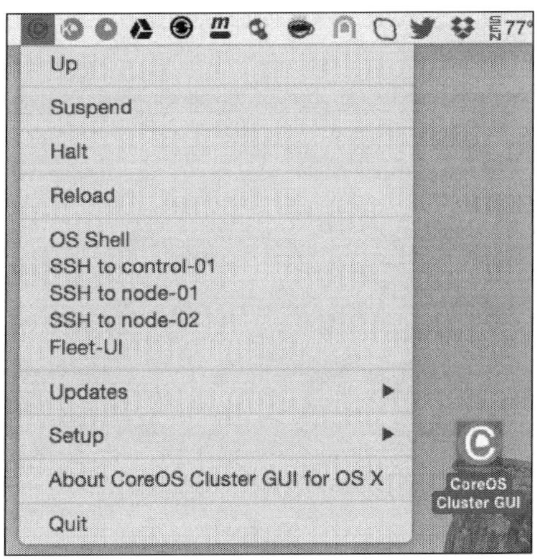

This app will set up a small `control+` two-node local cluster, which makes easier to test cluster things on local computer before pushing them to the cloud.

References

You can read more about the CoreOS cluster architectures that we used for the local and cloud test/staging setup at `https://coreos.com/docs/cluster-management/setup/cluster-architectures/`.

Summary

In this chapter, you learned how to set up a CoreOS local development environment and a remote test/staging cluster on GCE. We scheduled fleet units based on different metadata tags.

In the next chapter, we will see how to deploy code to our cloud servers.

6

Building a Deployment Setup

In the previous chapter, you learned how to set up a local CoreOS environment for development on a personal computer and a Test and Staging environment cluster on Google Cloud's Compute Engine VM instances.

In this chapter, we will cover how to deploy code from the GitHub repository to our Test and Staging servers, and how to set up the Docker builder and Docker private registry worker for Docker image building and distribution.

In this chapter, we will cover the following topics:

- Code deployment on Test and Staging servers
- Setting up the Docker builder and private Docker registry machine

Code deployment on Test and Staging servers

In the previous chapter, you learned how to set up your Test and Staging environment on Google Cloud and deploy your web servers there. In this section, we will see how to deploy code to our web servers on Test and Staging environments.

Deploying code on servers

To deploy code on our `Test1` and `Staging1` servers, we run the following commands:

```
$ cd coreos-essentials-book/chapter6/Test_Staging_Cluster/webserver
$ ./deploy_2_test1.sh
```

You will get this output:

```
Deploying code to tsc-test1 server !!!
index.html                                    100%  351     0.3KB/s   00:00

Finished !!!
Press [Enter] key to continue...
```

Then, run this command:

```
$ ./deploy_2_staging1.sh
```

You should see the following result:

```
Deploying code to tsc-staging1 server !!!
index.html                                    100%  354     0.4KB/s   00:00

Finished !!!
Press [Enter] key to continue...
```

Now open the `tsc-test1` and `tsc-staging1` VM instance external IPs, copying them to your browser (you can check out the IPs at GC Console, Compute Engine, VM Instance).

The output you see depends on the server.

For the Test server, you should see something like this:

This is what you will see for the Staging server:

Let's see what has happened here:

```
$ cat deploy_2_test1.sh
#!/bin/bash

function pause(){
read -p "$*"
}

## Fetch GC settings
# project and zone
project=$(cat ~/coreos-tsc-gce/settings | grep project= | head -1 |
cut -f2 -d"=")
zone=$(cat ~/coreos-tsc-gce/settings | grep zone= | head -1 | cut -f2
-d"=")

# change folder permissions
gcloud compute --project=$project ssh  --zone=$zone "core@tsc-test1"
--command "sudo chmod -R 755 /home/core/share/"

echo "Deploying code to tsc-test1 server !!!"
gcloud compute copy-files test1/index.html tsc-test1:/home/core/share/
nginx/html --zone $zone --project $project

echo " "
echo "Finished !!!"
pause 'Press [Enter] key to continue...'
```

As you can see, we used `gcloud compute` to change the permissions for our `home/core/share/nginx/html` folder, as we need to be able to copy files there. We copied a single `index.html` file there.

In real-life scenarios, `git pull` should be used there to pull from the Test and Staging branches.

To automate releases to the `Test1/Staging1` servers, for example, Strider-CD can be used, but this is beyond the scope of this book. You can read about Strider-CD at `https://github.com/Strider-CD/strider` and practice implementing it.

Setting up the Docker builder and private Docker registry worker

We have successfully deployed code `(index.html` in our case) in our Test/Staging environment on the cloud with the help of `gcloud compute`, by running it in a simple shell script.

Let's set up a new server in our Test/Staging environment on the cloud. It will build Docker images for us and store them in our private Docker Registry so that they can be used on our production cluster (you will learn how to set this up in the next chapter).

Server setup

As both Docker builder and Private Docker Registry fleet units will run on the same server, we are going to deploy one more server on the Test/Staging environment.

To install a new server, run the following commands:

```
$ cd coreos-essentials-book/chapter6/Test_Staging_Cluster
$ ls
cloud-config
create_registry-cbuilder1.sh
dockerfiles
files
fleet
webserver
```

Next, let's install our new server:

```
$ ./create_ registry-cbuilder1.sh
```

You should see output similar to this:

```
Created [https://www.googleapis.com/compute/v1/projects/radiant-works-93210/zones/europe-west1-d/instances/tsc-registry-cbuilder1].
NAME                    ZONE           MACHINE_TYPE  PREEMPTIBLE INTERNAL_IP    EXTERNAL_IP    STATUS
tsc-registry-cbuilder1 europe-west1-d n1-standard-1             10.240.220.147 104.155.47.244 RUNNING
Created [https://www.googleapis.com/compute/v1/projects/radiant-works-93210/global/routes/ip-10-200-4-1-tsc-registry-cbuilder1].
NAME                                  NETWORK DEST_RANGE    NEXT_HOP                                         PRIORITY
ip-10-200-4-1-tsc-registry-cbuilder1 default 10.200.4.1/32 europe-west1-d/instances/tsc-registry-cbuilder1 1000

Setup has finished !!!
Press [Enter] key to continue...
```

Let's see what happened during the process of script installation:

- A new server tsc-registry-cbuilder1 was created
- The static IP's 10.200.4.1 forward route for the tsc-registry-cbuilder1 instance was created
- The external port 5000 was opened for the new server
- File reg-dbuilder1.sh from the files folder got copied to ~/coreos-tsc-gce/bin
- The dbuilder.service and registry.service fleet units from the fleet folder got copied to ~/coreos-tsc-gce/fleet

If we check out the GCE VM Instances at the GC console, we should see our new instance there:

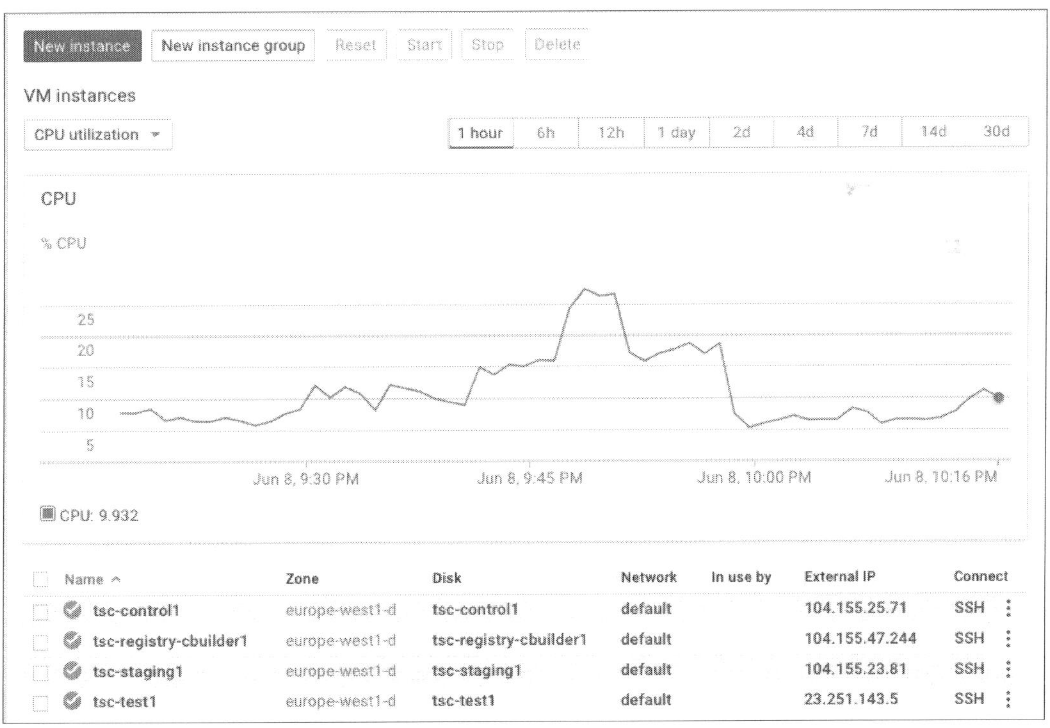

We now need to verify that our new server is working fine, so we perform `ssh` on it:

```
$ cd ~/coreos-tsc-gce/bin
$ ./reg-dbuider1.sh
```

```
CoreOS beta (681.0.0)
core@tsc-registry-cbuilder1 ~ $
```

Very good! Our new server is up-and-running. Press *Ctrl* + *D* to exit.

Now we need to verify that our server is connected to our cluster. So, run the following command:

```
$ ./set_cluster_access.sh
```

The script's output should look like this:

```
list fleet machines:
MACHINE         IP              METADATA
6c8af764...     10.240.222.1    cpeer=tsc-control1,role=services
b39dd6d6...     104.155.23.81   cpeer=tsc-staging1,role=worker
e06c9f74...     23.251.143.5    cpeer=tsc-test1,role=worker
f974daae...     104.155.47.244  cpeer=tsc-reg-cbuilder1,role=worker
list fleet units:
UNIT                            MACHINE                         ACTIVE  SUB
staging1_webserver.service      b39dd6d6.../104.155.23.81       active  running
test1_webserver.service         e06c9f74.../23.251.143.5        active  running
```

Perfect! We can see that our new server has successfully connected to our cluster:

```
f974daae...     104.155.47.244  cpeer=tsc-reg-cbuilder1,role=worker
```

Okay, now let's install those two new fleet units:

```
$ cd ~/coreos-tsc-gce/fleet
$ fleetctl start dbuilder.service registry.service
```

```
Unit dbuilder.service launched on f974daae.../104.155.47.244
Unit registry.service launched on f974daae.../104.155.47.244
```

Next, let's list the fleet units:

```
$ fleetctl list-units
```

```
UNIT                         MACHINE                        ACTIVE      SUB
dbuilder.service             f974daae.../104.155.47.244     activating  start-pre
registry.service             f974daae.../104.155.47.244     active      running
staging1_webserver.service   b39dd6d6.../104.155.23.81      active      running
test1_webserver.service      e06c9f74.../23.251.143.5       active      running
```

If you see `activating start-pre`, give the `fleet` units a few minutes to pull the remote Docker images.

You can check the status of the `fleet` units using the following command:

```
$ fleetctl status dbuilder.service
```

```
● dbuilder.service - docker-builder
   Loaded: loaded (/run/fleet/units/dbuilder.service; linked-runtime; vendor preset: disabled)
   Active: active (running) since Mon 2015-06-08 21:56:34 ; 3min 33s ago
  Process: 1479 ExecStartPre=/bin/sh -c /usr/bin/docker rm docker-builder (code=exited, status=1/FAILURE)
  Process: 1122 ExecStartPre=/bin/sh -c docker pull quay.io/rimusz/dbuilder:latest (code=exited, status=0/SUCCESS)
 Main PID: 1485 (docker)
   Memory: 4.5M
   CGroup: /system.slice/dbuilder.service
           └─1485 /usr/bin/docker run --rm --name docker-builder --hostname=tsc-registry-cbuilder1-docker-builder -p 2222:22 -v /home/core/.
ssh/authorized_keys:/tmp/authorized_keys -v /home/core/data:/data -v /var/run/docker.sock:/var/run/docker.sock -v /usr/bin/docker:/usr/bin/d
ocker -v /usr/lib/libdevmapper.so.1.02:/usr/lib/libdevmapper.so.1.02 quay.io/rimusz/dbuilder:latest

Jun 08 21:56:34 tsc-registry-cbuilder1.c.radiant-works-93210.internal sh[1485]: *** Running /etc/my_init.d/00_regen_ssh_host_keys.sh...
Jun 08 21:56:34 tsc-registry-cbuilder1.c.radiant-works-93210.internal sh[1485]: No SSH host key available. Generating one...
Jun 08 21:56:34 tsc-registry-cbuilder1.c.radiant-works-93210.internal sh[1485]: Creating SSH2 RSA key; this may take some time ...
Jun 08 21:56:34 tsc-registry-cbuilder1.c.radiant-works-93210.internal sh[1485]: Creating SSH2 DSA key; this may take some time ...
Jun 08 21:56:34 tsc-registry-cbuilder1.c.radiant-works-93210.internal sh[1485]: Creating SSH2 ECDSA key; this may take some time ...
Jun 08 21:56:34 tsc-registry-cbuilder1.c.radiant-works-93210.internal sh[1485]: Creating SSH2 ED25519 key; this may take some time ...
Jun 08 21:56:35 tsc-registry-cbuilder1.c.radiant-works-93210.internal sh[1485]: invoke-rc.d: policy-rc.d denied execution of restart.
Jun 08 21:56:35 tsc-registry-cbuilder1.c.radiant-works-93210.internal sh[1485]: *** Running /etc/rc.local...
Jun 08 21:56:35 tsc-registry-cbuilder1.c.radiant-works-93210.internal sh[1485]: *** Booting runit daemon...
Jun 08 21:56:35 tsc-registry-cbuilder1.c.radiant-works-93210.internal sh[1485]: *** Runit started as PID 98
```

Suppose we try again in a couple of minutes:

```
$ fleetctl list-units
```

```
UNIT                         MACHINE                        ACTIVE  SUB
dbuilder.service             f974daae.../104.155.47.244     active  running
registry.service             f974daae.../104.155.47.244     active  running
staging1_webserver.service   b39dd6d6.../104.155.23.81      active  running
test1_webserver.service      e06c9f74.../23.251.143.5       active  running
```

Then we can see that we've successfully got two new `fleet` units on our new `tsc-registry-cbuilder1` server.

You might remember from the previous chapter that the `set_cluster_access.sh` script does the following:

- It sets `PATH` to the `~/coreos-tsc-gce/bin` folder so that we can access executable files and scripts stored there from any folder
- It sets `FLEETCTL_TUNNEL` to our `control/etcd` machine's external IP
- It prints machines at the cluster with `fleetctl list-machines`
- It prints units at the cluster with `fleetctl list-units`
- It allows us to work with a remote `etcd` cluster via a local `fleetctl` client

Summary

In this chapter, you learned how to deploy code on a remote Test/Staging cluster on GCE, and set up the Docker builder and private Docker registry machine.

In the following chapter, we will cover these topics: using our Staging and Docker builder and private registry servers to deploy code from Staging to production, building Docker images, and deploying them on production servers.

7
Building a Production Cluster

In the previous chapter, we saw how to deploy code on a remote test/staging cluster, and set up the Docker builder and Private Docker Registry server. In this chapter, we will cover how to set up a production cluster on Google Cloud Compute Engine and how to deploy code from the Staging server using the Docker builder and Docker private registry.

We will cover the following topics in this chapter:

- Bootstrapping a remote Production cluster to GCE
- Deploying code on the Production cluster servers
- An overview of the setup of Dev/Test/Staging/Production
- PaaS based on `fleet`
- Another cloud alternative to run CoreOS clusters

Bootstrapping a remote production cluster on GCE

We have already seen how to set up our test/staging environment on Google Cloud. Here, we will use a very similar approach to set up our Production cluster, where the usually tested code is run in a stable environment with more powerful and high-availability servers.

Setting up the production cluster

Before we install the cluster, let's see what folders/files we have there; type the following commands in your terminal:

```
$ cd coreos-essentials-book/chapter7/Production_Cluster
$ ls
cloud-config
create_cluster_workers.sh
fleet
files
create_cluster_control.sh
install_fleetctl_and_scripts.sh
settings
```

As you can see, we have folders/files that are very similar to what we used to set up the Test/Staging Cluster.

> We are not going to print all the scripts and files that we are going to use, as it will take up half the chapter just for that. Take a look at the scripts and other files. They are very well-commented, and it should not be too difficult to understand them.

When you are done with this chapter, you can adopt the provided scripts to bootstrap your clusters. As before, update the `settings` file with your Google Cloud project ID and the zone where you want CoreOS instances to be deployed:

1. Next let's install our control server, which is our Production cluster's etcd node:

   ```
   $ ./create_cluster_control.sh
   ```

```
Created [https://www.googleapis.com/compute/v1/projects/radiant-works-93210/zones/europe-west1-c/instances/prod-control1].
NAME          ZONE           MACHINE_TYPE PREEMPTIBLE INTERNAL_IP   EXTERNAL_IP   STATUS
prod-control1 europe-west1-c g1-small                 10.240.22.131 130.211.87.34 RUNNING
Created [https://www.googleapis.com/compute/v1/projects/radiant-works-93210/global/routes/ip-10-220-1-1-prod-control1].
NAME                        NETWORK DEST_RANGE    NEXT_HOP                                 PRIORITY
ip-10-220-1-1-prod-control1 default 10.220.1.1/32 europe-west1-c/instances/prod-control1 1000

Setup has finished !!!
Press [Enter] key to continue...
```

We've just created our new Production cluster's control node.

For learning purposes, we used only one `etcd` server. For a real Production Cluster, a minimum of three `etcd` servers is recommended, and each server should be located in a different cloud availability zone.

As the Production cluster setup scripts are very similar to the Test/Staging cluster scripts, we are not going to analyze them here.

2. The next step is to create our Production cluster workers:

   ```
   $ ./create_cluster_workers.sh
   ```

   You should see the following output:

```
Created [https://www.googleapis.com/compute/v1/projects/radiant-works-93210/zones/europe-west1-c/instances/prod-web1]
NAME      ZONE           MACHINE_TYPE  PREEMPTIBLE INTERNAL_IP    EXTERNAL_IP   STATUS
prod-web1 europe-west1-c n1-standard-1             10.240.210.239 23.251.140.55 RUNNING
Created [https://www.googleapis.com/compute/v1/projects/radiant-works-93210/global/routes/ip-10-220-2-1-prod-web1].
NAME                    NETWORK DEST_RANGE    NEXT_HOP                                   PRIORITY
ip-10-220-2-1-prod-web1 default 10.220.2.1/32 europe-west1-c/instances/prod-web1 1000
```

   For the other cluster workers, you should see something like this:

```
Created [https://www.googleapis.com/compute/v1/projects/radiant-works-93210/zones/europe-west1-c/instances/prod-web2]
NAME      ZONE           MACHINE_TYPE  PREEMPTIBLE INTERNAL_IP   EXTERNAL_IP   STATUS
prod-web2 europe-west1-c n1-standard-1             10.240.189.53 130.211.53.11 RUNNING
Created [https://www.googleapis.com/compute/v1/projects/radiant-works-93210/global/routes/ip-10-220-3-1-prod-web2].
NAME                    NETWORK DEST_RANGE    NEXT_HOP                                   PRIORITY
ip-10-220-3-1-prod-web2 default 10.220.3.1/32 europe-west1-c/instances/prod-web2 1000
```

> Make a note of the workers' external IPs; we will need them later. Of course, you can always check them out at the Google Cloud Developers Console.

So, we've got our production servers set up on GCE. If you check out the Google Cloud Developers Console for Compute Engine Instances, you should see a list of servers, like this:

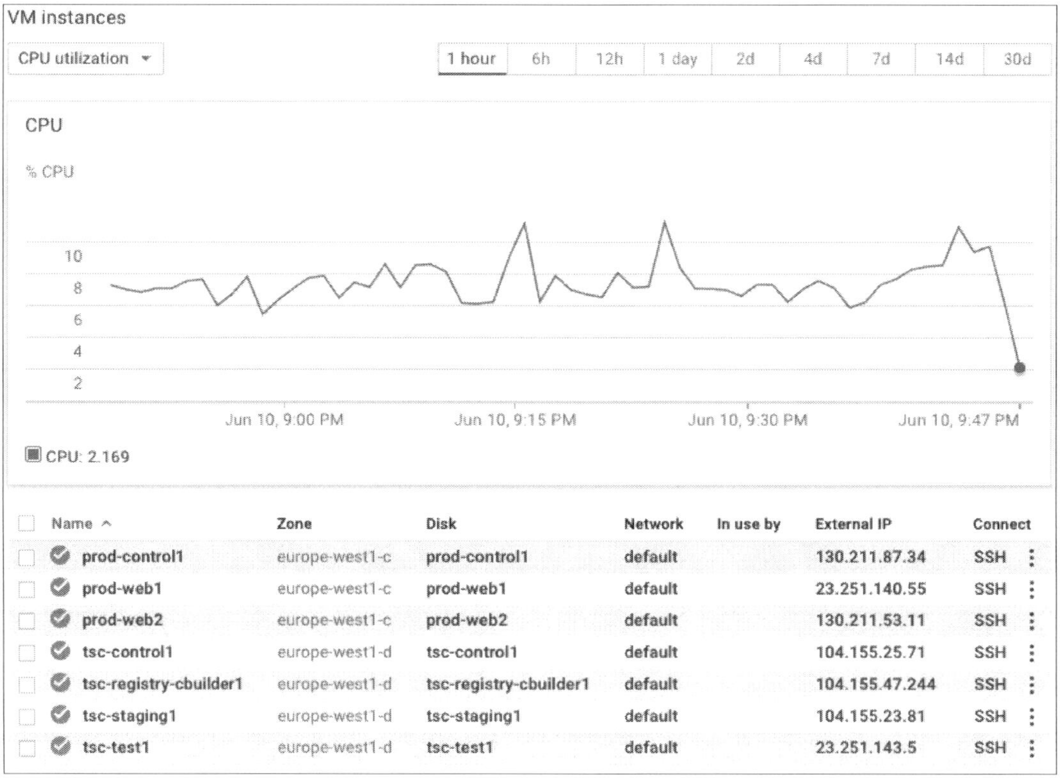

3. Now let's install all the necessary scripts to access our cluster:

   ```
   $ ./install_fleetctl_and_scripts.sh
   ```

   This script will create a new folder called `~/coreos-prod-gce`, which will have the same folders as our Test/Staging cluster:

   - The `bin` folder will have scripts for accessing cluster machines and the `set_cluster_access.sh` script
   - The `fleet - website1.service fleet` unit file

4. Let's run `set_cluster_access.sh`:

```
$ cd ~/coreos-prod-gce/bin
$ ./set_cluster_access.sh
```

```
bash-3.2$ ./set_cluster_access.sh
list fleet machines:
MACHINE         IP              METADATA
22002dc6...     10.240.174.222  cpeer=prod-web2,role=worker,service=website1
8ea105d5...     10.240.144.189  cpeer=prod-web1,role=worker,service=website1
b2bf842b...     10.240.148.108  cpeer=prod-control1,role=services
list fleet units:
UNIT    MACHINE ACTIVE  SUB
bash-3.2$
```

Perfect! Our production cluster is up-and-running!

As you can see, we have three servers there, one for the `etcd` services and two workers to run our website.

We already have the `website1 fleet` unit prepared. Let's install it:

```
$ cd ~/coreos-prod-gce/fleet
$ fleetctl start website1.service
```

The following screenshot demonstrates the output:

```
UNIT                    MACHINE                         ACTIVE
website1.service        32547c5c.../23.251.140.55       activating
website1.service        5764519e.../130.211.53.11       activating
```

Now we are ready to deploy code on our Production servers.

Deploying code on production cluster servers

In the previous chapters, we saw how to set up our Test/Staging environment on Google Cloud and deploy our code there, and we did set up our Docker builder and Docker Private Registry server.

In the next section, we will learn how to deploy code on our Web servers in Production cluster using Docker builder and Docker Private Registry.

Setting up the Docker builder server

Before we deploy our code from staging to production, we need to copy the `Dockerfile` and the `build.sh` and `push.sh` files to our Docker builder.

To do this, run the following commands:

```
$ cd coreos-essentials-book/chapter7/Test_Staging_Cluster/
$ ./install_website1_2_dbuilder.sh
```

You should see something like what is shown in the following screenshot:

```
Deploy docker image building script to tsc-registry-cbuilder1 server !!!
Dockerfile                                          100%   85     0.1KB/s   00:00
build.sh                                            100%   48     0.1KB/s   00:00
push.sh                                             100%   37     0.0KB/s   00:00

Finished !!!
Press [Enter] key to continue...
```

So let's check out what happened—that is, what that script has done. It has copied three files to Docker builder server:

1. This will be used to build our production Docker image:

   ```
   $ cat Dockerfile:
   FROM nginx:latest
   ## add website code
   ADD website1 /usr/share/nginx/html
   EXPOSE 80
   ```

2. The following is the Docker image building script:

   ```
   $ cat build.sh
   docker build --rm -t 10.200.4.1:5000/website1 .
   ```

3. Here is the Docker image push script to our Private Docker Registry:

   ```
   $ cat push.sh
   docker push 10.200.4.1:5000/website1
   ```

Okay, we have prepared our Docker builder server. Let's start cracking the code deployment on the production servers.

Deploying code on production servers

To deploy code on our production web servers, run the following command:

```
$ cd ~/coreos-prod-gce
```

When we built the production cluster, the install script installed the `deploy_2_production_website1.sh` script. Let's run it, and you should see an output similar to the next two screenshots:

```
$ ./deploy_2_production_website1.sh
```

```
receiving incremental file list
./
index.html

sent 46 bytes  received 330 bytes  752.00 bytes/sec
total size is 354  speedup is 0.94
Build new docker image and push to registry!!!
Sending build context to Docker daemon 5.632 kB
Sending build context to Docker daemon
Step 0 : FROM nginx:latest
 ---> a785ba7493fd
Step 1 : ADD website1 /usr/share/nginx/html
 ---> 174b9848dad1
Removing intermediate container a0b983d11f16
Step 2 : EXPOSE 80
 ---> Running in 0613dee11b3a
 ---> 8ff16c1dac76
Removing intermediate container 0613dee11b3a
Successfully built 8ff16c1dac76
The push refers to a repository [10.200.4.1:5000/website1] (len: 1)
Sending image list
Pushing repository 10.200.4.1:5000/website1 (1 tags)
Image dc2e1697e33e already pushed, skipping
Image df2a0347c9d0 already pushed, skipping
Image 39bb80489af7 already pushed, skipping
Image e21d523a1481 already pushed, skipping
Image 1f1cfc8b4072 already pushed, skipping
Image 8cac0c007422 already pushed, skipping
Image 3ec5f57e729c already pushed, skipping
Image 5ec936b59c11 already pushed, skipping
Image 72d73c46937a already pushed, skipping
Image a785ba7493fd already pushed, skipping
Image 514f4db63e53 already pushed, skipping
Image e2fde5e7e71f already pushed, skipping
174b9848dad1: Pushing
174b9848dad1: Buffering to disk
174b9848dad1: Image successfully pushed
8ff16c1dac76: Pushing
8ff16c1dac76: Buffering to disk
8ff16c1dac76: Image successfully pushed
Pushing tag for rev [8ff16c1dac76] on {http://10.200.4.1:5000/v1/repositories/website1/tags/latest}
```

You should also see something like this:

```
Status: Image is up to date for 10.200.4.1:5000/website1:latest
Pull new docker image on web2
Pulling repository 10.200.4.1:5000/website1
ccb82d095568: Pulling image (latest) from 10.200.4.1:5000/website1
ccb82d095568: Pulling image (latest) from 10.200.4.1:5000/website1, endpoint: http://10.200.4.1:5000/v1
ccb82d095568: Pulling dependent layers
39bb80489af7: Download complete
df2a0347c9d0: Download complete
dc2e1697e33e: Download complete
e21d523a1481: Download complete
5ec936b59c11: Download complete
3ec5f57e729c: Download complete
1f1cfc8b4072: Download complete
514f4db63e53: Download complete
e2fde5e7e71f: Download complete
8cac0c007422: Download complete
72d73c46937a: Download complete
a785ba7493fd: Download complete
b658f83182e7: Download complete
ccb82d095568: Download complete
ccb82d095568: Download complete
Status: Image is up to date for 10.200.4.1:5000/website1:latest
Restart fleet unit
Triggered global unit website1.service stop
Triggered global unit website1.service start

List Production cluster fleet units
UNIT                    MACHINE                         ACTIVE  SUB
website1.service        32547c5c.../23.251.140.55       active  running
website1.service        5764519e.../130.211.53.11       active  running

Finished !!!
Press [Enter] key to continue...
```

Now open `prod-web1` and `prod-web2` in your browser using their external IPs, and you should see something like what is shown in the following screenshot:

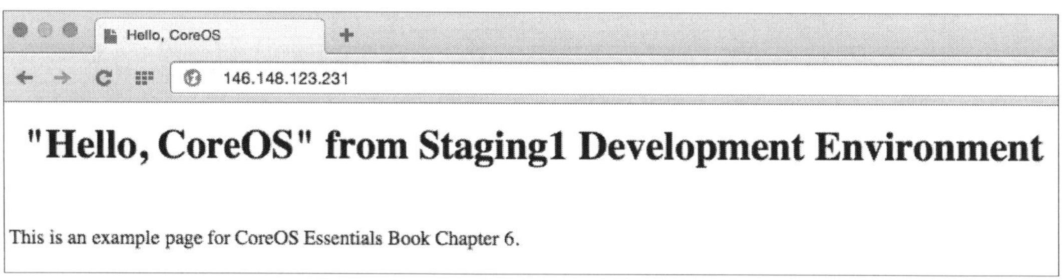

We see exactly the same web page as on our staging server.

Awesome! Our deployment to production servers is working fine!

Let's see what happened there.

Run the following command:

```
$ cat deploy_2_production_website1.sh
#!/bin/bash
# Build docker container for website1
# and release it

function pause(){
read -p "$*"
}

# Test/Staging cluster
## Fetch GC settings
# project and zone
project=$(cat ~/coreos-tsc-gce/settings | grep project= | head -1 | cut
-f2 -d"=")
zone=$(cat ~/coreos-tsc-gce/settings | grep zone= | head -1 | cut -f2
-d"=")
cbuilder1=$(gcloud compute instances list --project=$project | grep -v
grep | grep tsc-registry-cbuilder1 | awk {'print $5'})

# create a folder on docker builder
echo "Entering dbuilder docker container"
ssh -o UserKnownHostsFile=/dev/null -o StrictHostKeyChecking=no
core@$cbuilder1 "/usr/bin/docker exec docker-builder /bin/bash -c 'sudo
mkdir -p /data/website1 && sudo chmod -R 777 /data/website1'"

# sync files from staging to docker builder
echo "Deploying code to docker builder server !!!"
ssh -o UserKnownHostsFile=/dev/null -o StrictHostKeyChecking=no
core@$cbuilder1 '/usr/bin/docker exec docker-builder rsync -e "ssh -o
UserKnownHostsFile=/dev/null -o StrictHostKeyChecking=no" -avzW --delete
core@10.200.3.1:/home/core/share/nginx/html/ /data/website1'
# change folder permisions to 755
ssh -o UserKnownHostsFile=/dev/null -o StrictHostKeyChecking=no
core@$cbuilder1 "/usr/bin/docker exec docker-builder /bin/bash -c 'sudo
chmod -R 755 /data/website1'"

echo "Build new docker image and push to registry!!!"
ssh -o UserKnownHostsFile=/dev/null -o StrictHostKeyChecking=no
core@$cbuilder1 "/usr/bin/docker exec docker-builder /bin/bash -c 'cd /
```

```
data && ./build.sh && ./push.sh'"
##

# Production cluster
## Fetch GC settings
# project and zone
project2=$(cat ~/coreos-prod-gce/settings | grep project= | head -1 | cut
-f2 -d"=")

# Get servers IPs
control1=$(gcloud compute instances list --project=$project2 | grep -v
grep | grep prod-control1 | awk {'print $5'})
web1=$(gcloud compute instances list --project=$project2 | grep -v grep |
grep prod-web1 | awk {'print $5'})
web2=$(gcloud compute instances list --project=$project2 | grep -v grep |
grep prod-web2 | awk {'print $5'})

echo "Pull new docker image on web1"
ssh -o UserKnownHostsFile=/dev/null -o StrictHostKeyChecking=no
core@$web1 docker pull 10.200.4.1:5000/website1
echo "Pull new docker image on web2"
ssh -o UserKnownHostsFile=/dev/null -o StrictHostKeyChecking=no
core@$web2 docker pull 10.200.4.1:5000/website1

echo "Restart fleet unit"
# restart fleet unit
ssh -o UserKnownHostsFile=/dev/null -o StrictHostKeyChecking=no
core@$control1 fleetctl stop website1.service
ssh -o UserKnownHostsFile=/dev/null -o StrictHostKeyChecking=no
core@$control1 fleetctl start website1.service
#
sleep 5
echo " "
echo "List Production cluster fleet units"
ssh -o UserKnownHostsFile=/dev/null -o StrictHostKeyChecking=no
core@$control1 fleetctl list-units

echo " "
echo "Finished !!!"
pause 'Press [Enter] key to continue...'
```

The steps for deployment to production are as follows:

1. Creates a folder called `/data/website1` on the Docker builder server.
2. Use `rsync` via the docker-builder container to sync files from `Staging1` to the Docker builder server.
3. Run the `build.sh` script via the docker-builder container.
4. Push a new Docker image to the Private Docker Registry.
5. Pull a new Docker image onto the `Prod-web1` and `prod-web2` servers.
6. Restart the `website1.service fleet` unit via the Production cluster's `etcd` server.
7. And voilà! We have completed the release of a new website to our production cluster.

> **One thing to note**
>
> We are using the docker-builder container to sync and build our Docker container.
>
> This can be done directly on the Docker builder server, but using the container allows us to add any tools required to the container, which gives an advantage. If we need to replicate the Docker Builder server or replace it with a new one, we just have to install our docker-builder container to get things working again.

An overview of the Dev/Test/Staging/ Production setup

Let's overview the advantages of performing the setup of the Dev/Test/Staging/ Production environment in the way we did it:

- Local code development via the CoreOS VM decreases your testing time, as all changes get pushed to a local server on your VirtualBox VM.
- Cloud-based Test/Staging is good to use for team-shared projects using GitHub or Bitbucket. It also has, in our case, `nginx` containers running as our web servers, and the code is used via the attached `host` folder. This significantly speeds up code deployment from the test and staging `git` branches, as the Docker container does not need to be rebuilt each time we pull code from the `git` repository.

- For production, a separate cluster is used. It is good practice to separate development and production clusters.
- For production, we use the same Docker base image as that on the test/staging servers, but we build a new Docker image, with the code baked inside. So, we can, for example, auto-scale our website to as many servers as we want by reusing the same Docker image on all the servers, and all the servers will be running exactly the same code.
- For Docker image building and our Private Docker Registry, we use the same server, which is accessible only via the internal GCE IP. If you want to expose the Docker Registry to external access, for example, the `nginx` container with authentication should be put in front of the Docker registry to make it secure.
- This is only one way of setting up the Dev/Test/Staging/Production environment. Each setup scenario is different, but such setup should put you on the right path.

PaaS based on fleet

In this chapter and in previous chapters, we explained how to use fleet to deploy our different services on our clusters. Fleet is a powerful and easy-to-use low-level cluster manager that controls `systemd` at the cluster level. However, it lacks a web UI, easy orchestration tools, and so on, so this is where PAZ, the nice PaaS, steps in to help us out.

Deploying services using PAZ

The website at `http://www.paz.sh` has a very nice and user-friendly web UI, which makes it much easier to set up a CoreOS cluster. PAZ also has an API that you can use if you want to automate things via scripts.

Through its dashboard, you can add and edit your services, check the status of the cluster (viewed by host or by unit), and view monitoring information and logs for the cluster.

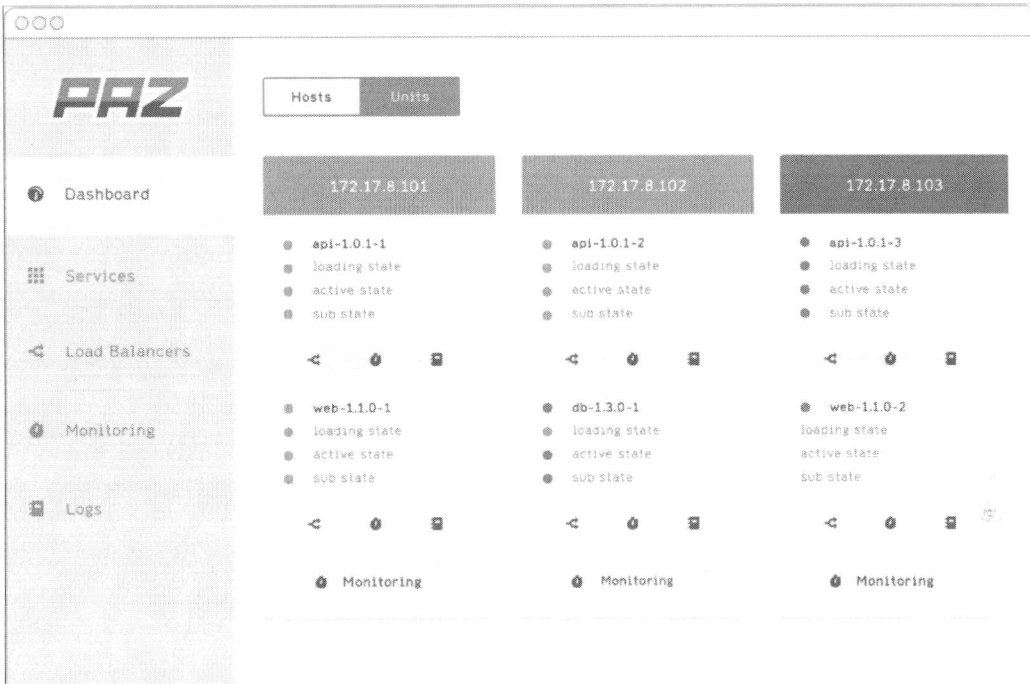

Paz Dashboard

It fully leverages `fleet` to orchestrate services across the machines in a cluster. It is built in `Node.js` and all its services run as Docker containers.

The following pointers explain how PAZ works:

- Users can declare services in the UI
- Services get stored in the service directory
- The scheduler is the service that deploys things
- You can manually tell the scheduler to deploy, or have it triggered at the end of your CI process
- Paz supports the post-push Docker Hub web hooks
- By using `etcd` and service discovery, your containers are linked together

Of course, it will keep evolving and getting new features but, at the time of writing this book, only the services in the preceding list were available.

Giving a complete overview of PAZ is beyond the scope of this book, but you can read more about the Paz architecture at `http://paz.readme.io/v1.0/docs/paz-architecture`.

Another cloud alternative for running CoreOS clusters

To bootstrap our Test/Staging and Production clusters, we used the Google Cloud Compute Engine's virtual instances, but sometimes you might want to run your servers on real servers (bare-metal servers) that are not stored at your premises.

There are a number of different bare-metal server providers out there, but one that caught my eye was `https://www.packet.net`.

I recently came across these while I was investigating hosting solutions for CoreOS and containers. They're interesting in the sense that, instead of going the typical cloud/hypervisor route, they've created a true, on-demand, and bare-metal cloud solution. I'm able to spin up a CoreOS server from scratch in less than 5 minutes, and they have a pretty comprehensive API and accompanying documentation.

Here's an example of a packet project dashboard:

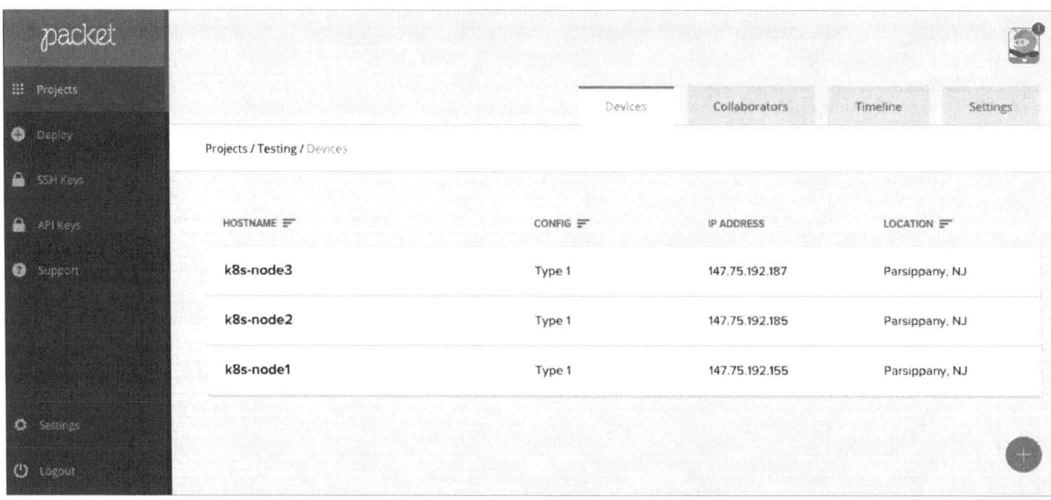

Summary

In this chapter, we saw how to set up a Production cluster and deploy our code staging using the Docker builder and private Docker registry machines. Finally, we overviewed a PaaS based on `fleet`—`Paz.sh`.

In the next chapter, we will overview the CoreOS update strategies and CoreUpdate for our servers. We will also make use of hosted public/private Docker repositories at `https://quay.io` and the self-hosted CoreOS Enterprise Registry.

8

Introducing CoreUpdate and Container/Enterprise Registry

In the previous chapter, we saw how to set up a production cluster and deploy our code, how to set up staging using Docker builder, and private Docker registry machines to production servers.

In this chapter, we will overview the CoreOS update strategies, paid CoreUpdate services, and Docker image hosting at the Container Registry and the Enterprise Registry.

In this chapter we will cover the following topics:

- Update strategies
- CoreUpdate
- Container Registry
- Enterprise Registry

Update strategies

Before we look at the paid CoreUpdate services from CoreOS, let's overview automatic update strategies that come out-of-the-box.

Automatic updates

CoreOS comes with automatic updates enabled by default.

As we have mentioned earlier, as updates are released by the CoreOS team, the host will stage them down to a temporary location and install to the passive `usr` partition. After rebooting, active and passive partitions get swapped.

At the time of writing this book, there are four update strategies, as follows:

STRATEGY	DESCRIPTION
`best-effort`	Default. If etcd is running, `etcd-lock`, otherwise simply `reboot`.
`etcd-lock`	Reboot after first taking a distributed lock in etcd.
`reboot`	Reboot immediately after an update is applied.
`off`	Do not reboot after updates are applied.

Which update strategy should be used is defined in the `update` part of `cloud-config`:

```
#cloud-config
coreos:
  update:
    group: stable
    reboot-strategy: best-effort
```

Let's take a look at what these update strategies are:

- `best-effort`: This is the default one and works in such a way that it checks whether the machine is part of the cluster. Then it uses `etcd-lock`; otherwise it uses the `reboot` strategy.
- `etcd-lock`: This allows us to boot only one machine at a time by putting a `reboot` lock on each machine and rebooting them one by one.
- `reboot`: This reboots the machine as soon as the update gets installed on the passive partition.
- `off`: The machine will not be rebooted after a successful update install onto the passive partition.

Uses of update strategies

Here are some examples of what `update` strategies can be used for:

- `best-effort`: This is recommended to be used in production clusters
- `reboot`: This can be used for machines that can only be rebooted at a certain time of the day—for example, for automatic updates in a maintenance window
- `off`: This can be used for a local development environment where the control of reboots is in the user's hands

If you want to learn more about update strategies, take a look at the CoreOS website at `https://coreos.com/docs/cluster-management/setup/update-strategies/`.

CoreUpdate

CoreUpdate is a part of the managed Linux plans (`https://coreos.com/products/`).

It is a tool in the commercial offerings of CoreOS. It provides users with their own supported Omaha server and is analogous to tools such as Red Hat Satellite Server and Canonical Landscape:

- The standard plan is managed and hosted by CoreOS
- The premium plan can be run behind the firewall, which can be on-premise or on the cloud

CoreUpdate uses exactly the same strategies as the aforementioned `update` strategies, except for a few differences in the `update` portion of the `cloud-config` file:

```
#cloud-config
  coreos:
    update:
      group: production
      server: https://customer.update.core-os.net/v1/update
```

Here:

- `group` is what you have set at your CoreUpdate dashboard
- `server` is the link generated for you after signing in for the managed Linux plan

In our current example, as per `cloud-config`, the servers belong to `https://customer.update.core-os.net/v1/update` and `group` is `production`.

We change via the CoreUpdate UI, as shown in the following screenshot:

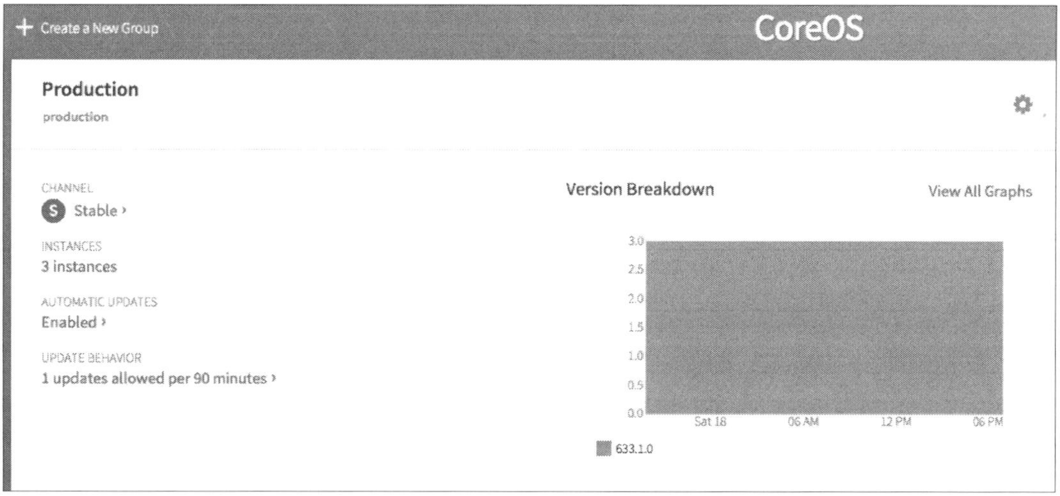

The following features are present:

- Release channel; in our case, it is the stable one
- Enable/disable automatic updates
- Time window between machines updates; in our case, it is 90 minutes

The CoreUpdate UI allows you to very easily control your cluster update groups, without any need to perform `ssh` via the terminal to your servers and change there on each server individually update settings.

> You can read more about CoreUpdate at the following pages:
>
> `https://coreos.com/docs/coreupdate/coreos/coreupdate-configure-machines`
>
> `https://coreos.com/docs/coreupdate/coreos/coreupdate-getting-started`

Container Registry

The Container Registry is a hosted CoreOS service for application containers at `https://quay.io`. There, you can host your Docker images if you don't want to run Private Docker Registry yourself:

- It offers free, unlimited storage and repositories for public container repositories
- If you want private repositories, it offers a plenty of plans to choose from

Quay.io overview

Let's go through an overview of what they have there: a nice and easy-to-use UI.

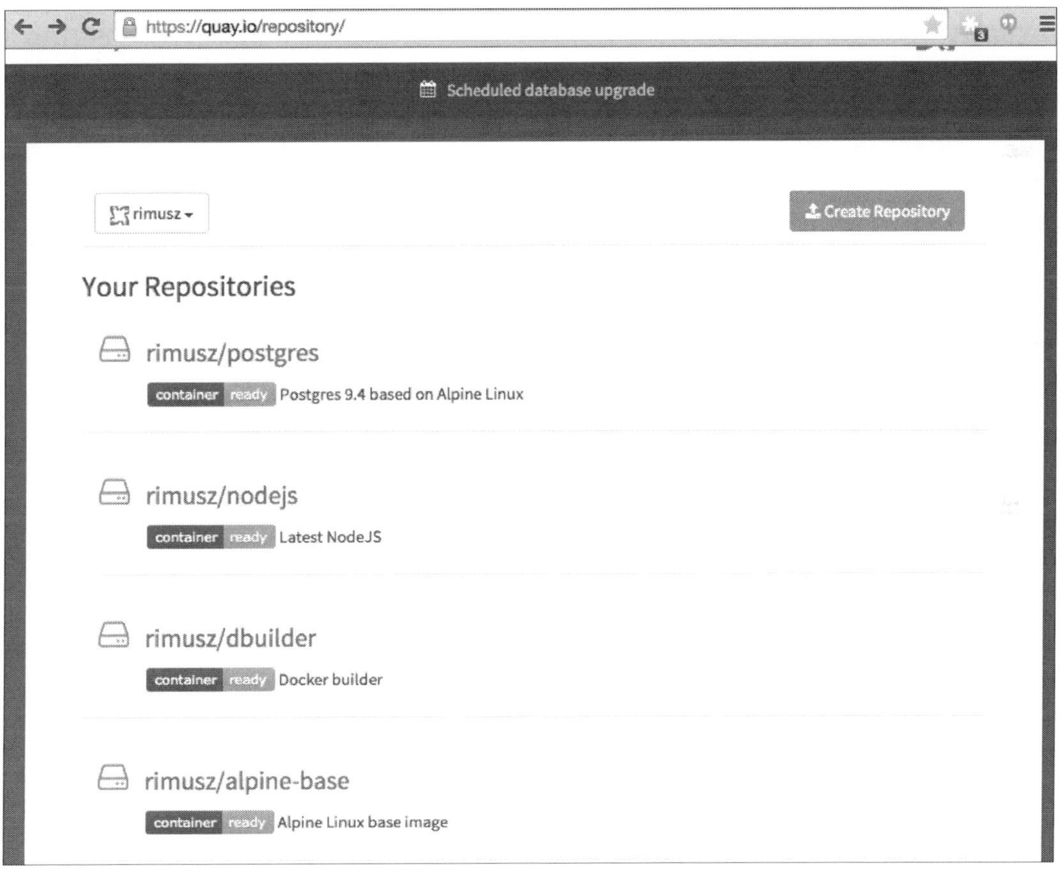

In the following screenshot we see postgres containers image in more details:

As you see from the preceding screenshot, the UI is very easy to use and it's easy to understand the features.

Let's see how the Create Repository feature looks:

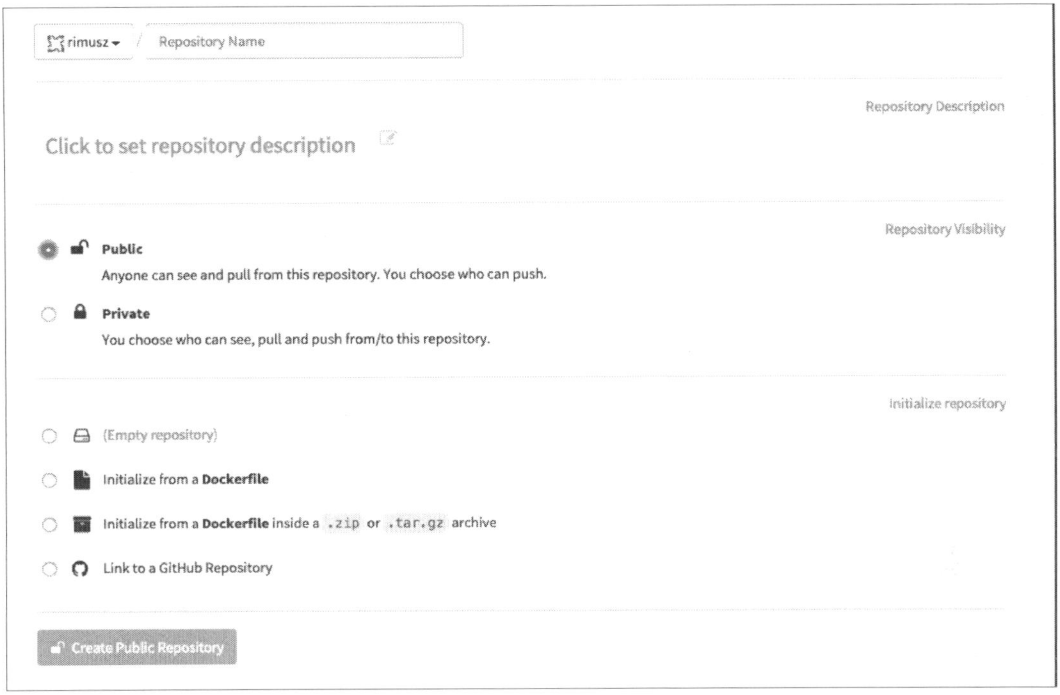

When you create a new repository, you can do the following:

- Make the repository public or private.
- Empty it if you want to build containers yourself and push them to the Registry.
- Provide (upload) a `Docker` file.
- Link to the GitHub repository. This is the preferred choice as it allows you to automate container building when you push changes to your GitHub Repository.

Enterprise Registry

Enterprise Registry is basically the same as Container Registry, but is hosted on your premises or cloud servers behind your firewall.

It has different plan options and can be found at `https://coreos.com/products/enterprise-registry/`.

It allows you to manage container builds, permissions of your teams and users, and so on.

If your company's requirement is a setup that is very secured and fully controlled by you, then using the Container Registry and Enterprise Registry is the way to go.

Summary

In this chapter, we overviewed the CoreOS update strategies, CoreUpdate services, the hosted free/paid Container Registry at `https://quay.io`, and the self-hosted Enterprise Registry services.

In the next chapter, you will be introduced to the CoreOS rkt—App Container runtime that can be used instead of Docker containers.

9
Introduction to CoreOS rkt

In the previous chapter, we overviewed CoreUpdate, free and paid container repositories, and the hosting and enterprise registry provided by CoreOS.

In this chapter, you will learn about CoreOS's `rkt`, a container runtime for applications. We will cover the following topics in this chapter:

- Introduction to `rkt`
- Running streamlined Docker images with `rkt`
- Converting Docker images to ACI

An introduction to rkt

rkt (pronounced "rock it") is a container runtime for applications made by CoreOS and is designed for composability, speed, and security. It is an alternative to Docker and is designed to be run on servers with the most rigorous security and production environments.

rkt is a standalone tool, compared to Docker's client and central daemon version, which makes it a better alternative to Docker, as it has fewer constraints and dependencies. For example, if the `docker` central daemon crashes, all running `docker` containers will be stopped; in the case of `rkt`, however, this can affect only the particular rkt process responsible for running `rkt` containers in its pod. As each `rkt` process gets its **process identification number** (**PID**), if one `rkt` process dies, it will not affect any other `rkt` process.

Features of rkt

We will overview the main `rkt` features, as follows:

- It can be integrated with `init` systems, as `systemd` and `upstart`
- It can be integrated with cluster orchestration tools, such as `fleet` and `Kubernetes` (which we will cover in the next chapter)
- It is compatible with other container solutions as Docker
- It has an extensible and modular architecture

The basics of App container

`rkt` is an implementation of **App Container** (**appc**: `https://github.com/appc/spec/`), which is open source and defines an image format, the runtime environment, and the discovery mechanism of application containers:

- `rkt` uses images of the **Application Container Image** (**ACI**) format as defined by the App Container (appc) specifications (`https://github.com/appc/spec`). An ACI is just a simple `tarball` bundle of different `rootfs` files and an image manifest.
- A pod (the basic unit of execution in `rkt`) is a grouping of one or more app images (ACIs), with some optionally applied additional metadata on the pod level—for example, applying some resource constraints, such as CPU usage.

Using rkt

As rkt comes preinstalled with CoreOS, running ACI images with rkt is easy and it is very similar to `docker` commands. (I would love to write more on this, but rkt does not provide many options yet, as it is constantly changing and innovating, which was also the case at the time of writing this book).

As `rkt` has no running OS X client, you need to log in to your CoreOS VM host directly to run the following example commands:

1. First, we need to trust the remote site before we download any ACI file from there, as `rkt` verifies signatures by default:

   ```
   $ sudo rkt trust -prefix example.com/nginx
   ```

2. Then we can fetch (download) an image from there:

   ```
   $ sudo rkt fetch example.com/nginx:latest
   ```

3. Then running the container with `rkt` is simple:

```
$ sudo rkt run example.com/nginx:v1.8.0
```

As you see, `rkt` appropriates ETags—as in our case v1.8.0 will be run.

rkt networking

By default `rkt` run uses the host mode for port assignments. For example, if you have `EXPOSE 80` in your Dockerfile, run this command:

```
$ sudo rkt run example.com/nginx:v1.8.0
```

The `rkt` pod will share the network stack and interfaces with the host machine.

If you want to assign a different port/private IP address, then use `run` with these parameters:

```
sudo rkt run --private-net --port=http:8000 example.com/nginx:v1.8.0
```

rkt environment variables

Environment variables can be inherited from the host using the `--inherit-env` flag. Using `flag --set-env`, we can set individual environment variables.

Okay, let's prepare a few environment variables to be inherited using these two commands:

```
$ export ENV_ONE=hi_from_host
$ export ENV_TWO=CoreOS
```

Now let's use them together with `--set-env` in the command, as follows:

```
$ sudo rkt run --inherit-env --set-env ENV_THREE=hi_nginx example.com/
nginx:v1.8.0
```

rkt volumes

For host volumes, the `-volume` flag needs to be used. Volumes need to be defined in the ACI manifest when creating the new ACI image and converting Docker images. You will get an output like this:

```
Converted volumes:
        name: "volume-/var/cache/nginx", path: "/var/cache/nginx", readOnly: false

Generated ACI(s):
nginx-latest.aci
```

The following command will mount the `host` directory on the `rkt` Pod:

```
$ sudo rkt run -volume volume-/var/cache/nginx,kind=host,source=/some_
folder/nginx_cache example.com/nginx:v1.8.0
```

Note that the `rkt` volume standard was not completed at the time of writing this book, so the previous example might not work when `rkt` reaches its final version.

Next let's see how `rkt` plays nicely with docker images.

Running streamlined Docker images with rkt

As there are thousands of docker images on the public Docker hub, `rkt` allows you to use them very easily. Alternatively, you might have some docker images and would like to run them with `rkt` too, without building new `rkt` ACI images, to see how they work with `rkt`.

Running Docker images is very much the same as it was in previous examples:

1. As Docker images do not support signature verification yet, we just skip the verification step and fetch one with the `--insecure-skip-verify` flag:

   ```
   $ sudo rkt --insecure-skip-verify fetch docker://nginx
   ```

```
rkt: fetching image from docker://nginx
Downloading layer: 3cb35ae859e76583ba7707df18ea7417e8d843682f4e5440a5279952c47fd8d8
Downloading layer: 41b730702607edf9b07c6098f0b704ff59c5d4361245e468c0d551f50eae6f84
Downloading layer: 97d05af69c4662fd1e4b177e7b91cbc8413a40e25a53f20408ccbc3b4fabb8b0
Downloading layer: 55516e2f25309bb5d153efe7da3a638566dff914bde0c418167ed39196fc3cbf
Downloading layer: 7ed37354d38dfee583c5f2dcc30b98f6537474e06c18a839a717e72094b72ac0
Downloading layer: e7e840eed70b58a5d1f172b72e24a83552932de6aad354036f4eced796ac0d32
Downloading layer: 0b5e8be9b692aa2a42f5bf9517b3da640718079006ccea923d1dab13e4d2df8e
Downloading layer: 439e7909f795b91a6b8c0520b204f0d50f5c4f02fe8af611502da09c583b5508
Downloading layer: ee8776c93fde95742b3777d5e743b603ebcc1f38d7565594848a1fde1c2963dd
Downloading layer: 50c46b6286b9a498aa767c9c3592e0a61ffee18fa3bea766e4ae33746226a47e
Downloading layer: e59ba510498bb53d2298ccc585b3140f4072f91070cd9b1c2bb504be87a4985b
Downloading layer: 42a3cf88f3f0cce2b4bfb2ed714eec5ee937525b4c7e0a0f70daff18c3f2ee92
sha512-13a9c5295d8c13b9ad94e37b25b2feb2
```

2. The last line shown in the preceding screenshot represents the `rkt` image ID of the converted ACI, and this can be used to `run` with `rkt` :

```
$ sudo rkt --insecure-skip-verify run sha512-13a9c5295d8c13b9ad94e
37b25b2feb2
```

3. Also we can run in this way, where the image will be downloaded and then run:

```
$ sudo rkt --insecure-skip-verify run docker://nginx
```

4. If we want to use volumes with Docker images, we run this line:

```
$ sudo rkt --insecure-skip-verify run \
--volume /home/core/share/nginx/html:/usr/share/nginx/html \
docker://nginx
```

   This is very similar to the `docker` command, isn't it?

5. Okay, let's update our local development `nginx.service` to use `rkt`:

```
[Unit]
Description=nginx
[Service]
User=root
TimeoutStartSec=0
EnvironmentFile=/etc/environment
ExecStart=/usr/bin/ rkt --insecure-skip-verify run \
 -volume /home/core/share/nginx/html:/usr/share/nginx/html \
docker://nginx
#
Restart=always
RestartSec=10s
[X-Fleet]
```

As you see, there is no `ExecStop=/usr/bin/docker stop nginx`. It is not needed because `systemd` takes care of stopping the `rkt` instance when the `systemctl`/`fleetctl` stop is used by sending the running `nginx` process a `SIGTERM`.

Much simpler than docker, right?

In the next section, we will see how to convert a docker image into an ACI image.

Converting Docker images into ACI

With CoreOS comes another file related to `rkt` — `docker2aci`. It converts a docker image to an ACI image (an application container image used by `rkt`).

Let's convert our `nginx` image. Run the following command:

```
$ docker2aci docker://nginx
```

```
Downloading layer: 3cb35ae859e76583ba7707df18ea7417e8d843682f4e5440a5279952c47fd8d8
Downloading layer: 41b730702607edf9b07c6098f0b704ff59c5d4361245e468c0d551f50eae6f84
Downloading layer: 97d05af69c4662fd1e4b177e7b91cbc8413a40e25a53f20408ccbc3b4fabb8b0
Downloading layer: 55516e2f25309bb5d153efe7da3a638566dff914bde0c418167ed39196fc3cbf
Downloading layer: 7ed37354d38dfee583c5f2dcc30b98f6537474e06c18a839a717e72094b72ac0
Downloading layer: e7e840eed70b58a5d1f172b72e24a83552932de6aad354036f4eced796ac0d32
Downloading layer: 0b5e8be9b692aa2a42f5bf9517b3da640718079006ccea923d1dab13e4d2df8e
Downloading layer: 439e7909f795b91a6b8c0520b204f0d50f5c4f02fe8af611502da09c583b5508
Downloading layer: ee8776c93fde95742b3777d5e743b603ebcc1f38d7565594848a1fde1c2963dd
Downloading layer: 50c46b6286b9a498aa767c9c3592e0a61ffee18fa3bea766e4ae33746226a47e
Downloading layer: e59ba510498bb53d2298ccc585b3140f4072f91070cd9b1c2bb504be87a4985b
Downloading layer: 42a3cf88f3f0cce2b4bfb2ed714eec5ee937525b4c7e0a0f70daff18c3f2ee92

Converted volumes:
        name: "volume-/var/cache/nginx", path: "/var/cache/nginx", readOnly: false

Generated ACI(s):
nginx-latest.aci
```

We can also save a docker image in a file and the convert it. Run the following command:

```
$ docker save -o nginx.docker nginx
$ docker2aci nginx.docker
```

```
Extracting layer: 3cb35ae859e76583ba7707df18ea7417e8d843682f4e5440a5279952c47fd8d8
Extracting layer: 41b730702607edf9b07c6098f0b704ff59c5d4361245e468c0d551f50eae6f84
Extracting layer: 97d05af69c4662fd1e4b177e7b91cbc8413a40e25a53f20408ccbc3b4fabb8b0
Extracting layer: 55516e2f25309bb5d153efe7da3a638566dff914bde0c418167ed39196fc3cbf
Extracting layer: 7ed37354d38dfee583c5f2dcc30b98f6537474e06c18a839a717e72094b72ac0
Extracting layer: e7e840eed70b58a5d1f172b72e24a83552932de6aad354036f4eced796ac0d32
Extracting layer: 0b5e8be9b692aa2a42f5bf9517b3da640718079006ccea923d1dab13e4d2df8e
Extracting layer: 439e7909f795b91a6b8c0520b204f0d50f5c4f02fe8af611502da09c583b5508
Extracting layer: ee8776c93fde95742b3777d5e743b603ebcc1f38d7565594848a1fde1c2963dd
Extracting layer: 50c46b6286b9a498aa767c9c3592e0a61ffee18fa3bea766e4ae33746226a47e
Extracting layer: e59ba510498bb53d2298ccc585b3140f4072f91070cd9b1c2bb504be87a4985b
Extracting layer: 42a3cf88f3f0cce2b4bfb2ed714eec5ee937525b4c7e0a0f70daff18c3f2ee92

Converted volumes:
        name: "volume-/var/cache/nginx", path: "/var/cache/nginx", readOnly: false

Generated ACI(s):
nginx-latest.aci
```

Finally, you can try to use the generated ACI files by updating the preceding `nginx.service` `fleet` unit:

```
[Unit]
Description=nginx
[Service]
User=root
TimeoutStartSec=0
EnvironmentFile=/etc/environment
ExecStart=/usr/bin/ rkt --insecure-skip-verify run \
 --volume volume-/usr/share/nginx/html,kind=host,source=/usr/share/nginx/
html \
 full_path_to/nginx-latest.aci
#
Restart=always
RestartSec=10s

 [X-Fleet]
```

Summary

In this chapter, we overviewed the main features of CoreOS rkt, the `rkt` application container, and the image format. You also learned how to run images based on `aci` and `docker` as containers with `rkt`.

In the next chapter, you will get an introduction to Google Kubernetes, an open source orchestration system for application containers.

10
Introduction to Kubernetes

In this chapter, we will cover a short overview of Google Kubernetes, which manages containerized applications across multiple hosts in a cluster. As Kubernetes is a very large project, in this chapter, we will only overview its main concepts and some use cases, including these:

- What is Kubernetes?
- Primary components of Kubernetes
- Kubernetes cluster setup
- Tectonic—CoreOS and Kubernetes combined for a commercial implementation

What is Kubernetes?

Google has been running everything in containers for more than decade. Internally, they use a system called Borg (`http://research.google.com/pubs/pub43438.html`), the predecessor of Kubernetes, to scale and orchestrate containers across servers.

Lessons learned from Borg were used to build Kubernetes, an open source container orchestration system. It became popular very quickly when it was released in June 2014.

All of the best ideas from Borg were incorporated into Kubernetes. Many of Borg's developers now work on Kubernetes.

Kubernetes received thousands of stars at it's GitHub project (`https://github.com/GoogleCloudPlatform/kubernetes`), and hundreds of supporters from the open source community and companies such as CoreOS, Red Hat, Microsoft, VMware, and so on.

Primary components of Kubernetes

Kubernetes can be run on any modern Linux operating system.

Here are the main components of Kubernetes:

- **Master**: This is the set of main Kubernetes control services, usually running on one server except the `etcd` cluster. However it can be spread around a few servers. The services of Kubernetes are as follows:
    - `etcd` cluster
    - API server
    - Controller manager
    - Scheduler
- **Node**: This is a cluster worker. It can be a VM and/or bare-metal server. Nodes are managed from the master services and are dedicated to run pods. These two Kubernetes services must run on each node:
    - Kubelet
    - Network proxy

  Docker and rkt are used to run application containers. In future, we will see more support for application container systems there.
- **Pod**: This is a group of application containers running with the shared context. Even a single application container must run in a Pod.
- **Replication controllers**: These ensure that the specified numbers of pods are running. If there are too many pods, will be killed. If they are too less, then the required number of pods will be started. It is not recommended to run pods without replication controllers even if there is a single Pod.
- **Services**: The same pod can be run only once. If it dies, the replication controller replaces it with a new pod. Every pod gets its own dedicated IP, which allows on the same node to run many containers on the port. But every time a pod is started from the template by replication controller gets a different IP, and this is where services come to help. Each service gets assigned a virtual IP, which stays with it until it dies.
- **Labels**: These are the arbitrary key-value pairs that are used by every Kubernetes component; for example, the replication controller uses them for service discovery.

- **Volumes**: A volume is a directory that is accessible from a container, and is used to store the container's stateful data.
- **Kubectl**: This controls the Kubernetes cluster manager. For example, you can add/delete nodes, pods, or replication controllers; check their status; and so on. Kubernetes uses `manifest` files to set up pods, replication controllers, services, labels, and so on.

Kubernetes has a nice UI, which was built and contributed to by `http://kismatic.io/`. It runs on an API server:

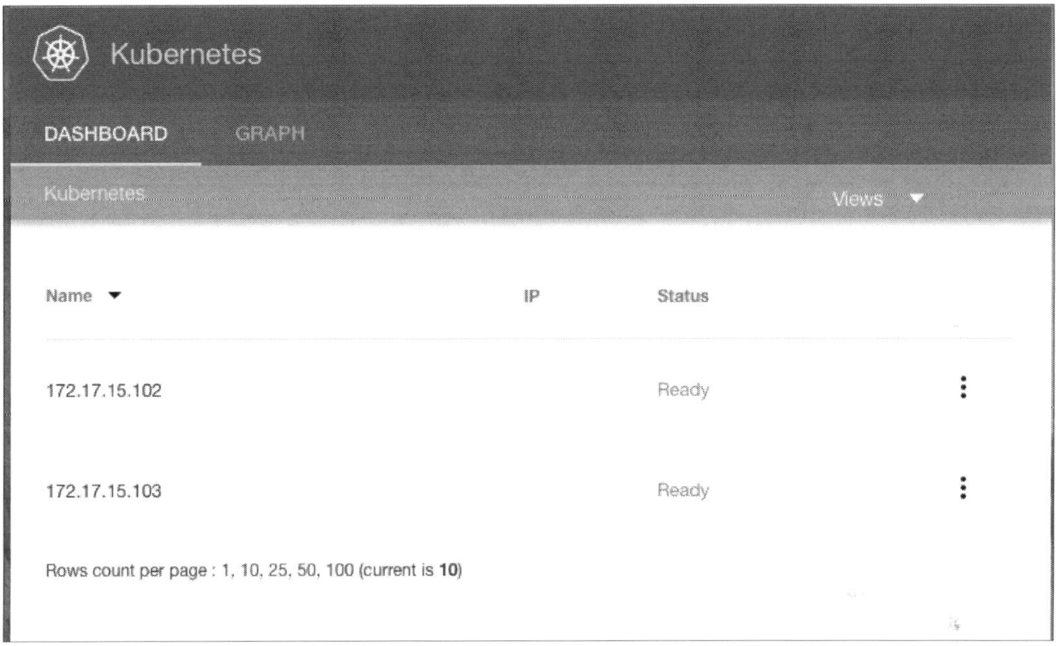

This allows us to check the Kubernetes cluster's status and add/delete pods, replication controllers, and so on. It also allows us to manage a Kubernetes cluster from the UI in the same way as from `kubectl`.

`http://kismatic.io/` is also going to offer an enterprise/commercial version of Kubernetes in the near future.

Kubernetes cluster setup

In the previous topic, we overviewed the main features of Kubernetes, so let's do some interesting stuff—installing small Kubernetes on Google Cloud.

Note, that if you are using a free/trial Google Cloud account, which has a limit of eight CPUs (eight VMs are allowed), you need to delete some of them. Let's replace our production cluster with a Kubernetes cluster. Select the VMs as per what is shown in the following screenshot. Then click on the **Delete** button in the top-right corner.

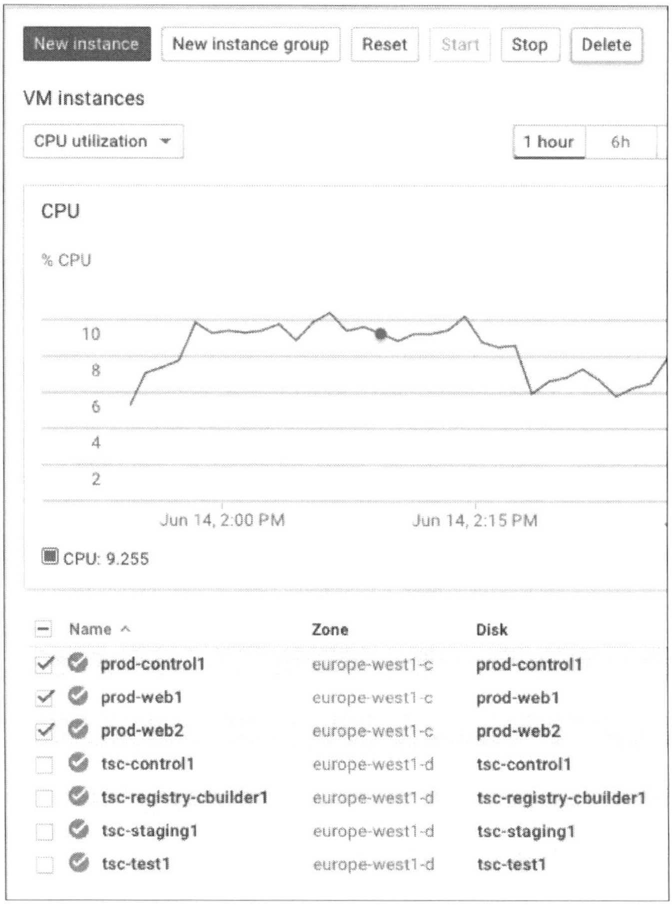

Now we are ready to install a Kubernetes cluster:

1. Type this in your terminal:

```
$ cd coreos-essentials-book/Chapter10/Kubernetes_Cluster
```

Note that as we have folders/files that are very similar to what we used to set up the Test/Staging/Production clusters, we are not going to review the scripts this time. You can always check out the setup files yourself and learn the differences there:

2. Update the `settings` file there with your GC project ID and zone.
3. Let's now run the first script, named `1-bootstrap_cluster.sh`:

   ```
   $ ./ 1-bootstrap_cluster.sh
   ```

   You should see an output similar to this:

```
Created [https://www.googleapis.com/compute/v1/projects/radiant-works-93210/zones/europe-west1-c/instances/k8s-master]
NAME       ZONE           MACHINE_TYPE PREEMPTIBLE INTERNAL_IP   EXTERNAL_IP   STATUS
k8s-master europe-west1-c g1-small                 10.240.48.137 23.251.140.55 RUNNING
Created [https://www.googleapis.com/compute/v1/projects/radiant-works-93210/global/routes/ip-10-222-1-1-k8s-master].
NAME                     NETWORK DEST_RANGE    NEXT_HOP                              PRIORITY
ip-10-222-1-1-k8s-master default 10.222.1.1/32 europe-west1-c/instances/k8s-master 1000
Created [https://www.googleapis.com/compute/v1/projects/radiant-works-93210/zones/europe-west1-c/instances/k8s-node-1]
NAME       ZONE           MACHINE_TYPE  PREEMPTIBLE INTERNAL_IP   EXTERNAL_IP   STATUS
k8s-node-1 europe-west1-c n1-standard-1             10.240.235.6 130.211.53.11 RUNNING
Created [https://www.googleapis.com/compute/v1/projects/radiant-works-93210/zones/europe-west1-c/instances/k8s-node-2]
NAME       ZONE           MACHINE_TYPE  PREEMPTIBLE INTERNAL_IP   EXTERNAL_IP    STATUS
k8s-node-2 europe-west1-c n1-standard-1             10.240.32.39 23.251.136.164 RUNNING

Cluster machines setup has finished !!!
```

If you check out the Google Cloud console, you should see three new VMs there, namely **k8s-master**, **k8s-node1**, and **k8s-node2**:

Name ^	Zone	Disk	Network	In use by	External IP	Connect
k8s-master	europe-west1-c	k8s-master	default		23.251.140.55	SSH
k8s-node-1	europe-west1-c	k8s-node-1	default		130.211.53.11	SSH
k8s-node-2	europe-west1-c	k8s-node-2	default		23.251.136.164	SSH
tsc-control1	europe-west1-d	tsc-control1	default		104.155.25.71	SSH
tsc-registry-cbuilder1	europe-west1-d	tsc-registry-cbuilder1	default		104.155.47.244	SSH
tsc-staging1	europe-west1-d	tsc-staging1	default		104.155.23.81	SSH
tsc-test1	europe-west1-d	tsc-test1	default		23.251.143.5	SSH

The `1-bootstrap_cluster.sh` script has installed a small CoreOS cluster, which is set up in the same way as our previous Test/Staging/Production cluster—one `etcd` server and two workers connected to it. And also create a new folder, `k8s-cluster`, in the user home folder where the `settings` file got copied and other binary files will be copied later on.

4. Next, we need to install the `fleetctl`, `etcdctl`, and `kubectl` local clients on our computer to be able to communicate with the CoreOS cluster `etcd` and `fleet` services, and with the Kubernetes master service.

   Type the following line in your terminal:

   ```
   $ ./2-get_k8s_fleet_etcd.sh
   ```

   You should see an output similar to this:

```
Downloading and instaling fleetctl, etcdctl and kubectl ...
Downloading etcdctl v2.0.11 for OS X
  % Total    % Received % Xferd  Average Speed   Time    Time     Time  Current
                                 Dload  Upload   Total   Spent    Left  Speed
100   409    0   409    0     0    361      0 --:--:--  0:00:01 --:--:--   361
100 5042k  100 5042k    0     0  1618k      0  0:00:03  0:00:03 --:--:-- 4775k
Archive:  etcd.zip
  inflating: etcdctl
etcdctl was copied to ~/k8s-cluster/bin

Downloading fleetctl v0.10.1 for OS X
  % Total    % Received % Xferd  Average Speed   Time    Time     Time  Current
                                 Dload  Upload   Total   Spent    Left  Speed
100   408    0   408    0     0    656      0 --:--:-- --:--:-- --:--:--   655
100 2483k  100 2483k    0     0  1110k      0  0:00:02  0:00:02 --:--:-- 3251k
Archive:  fleet.zip
  inflating: fleetctl
fleetctl was copied to ~/k8s-cluster/bin

Downloading kubernetes v0.19.0 kubectl for OS X
  % Total    % Received % Xferd  Average Speed   Time    Time     Time  Current
                                 Dload  Upload   Total   Spent    Left  Speed
100 18.9M  100 18.9M    0     0  6509k      0  0:00:02  0:00:02 --:--:-- 6508k

kubectl was copied to ~/k8s-cluster/bin


Instaling of fleetctl, etcdctl and kubectl has finished !!!
```

5. Now let's install the Kubernetes cluster on top our new CoreOS cluster.

   Type this command in your terminal:

   ```
   $ ./3-install_k8s_fleet_units.sh
   ```

You should see an output similar to what is shown here:

```
Kubernetes v0.19.0 will be installed ...
Unit kube-apiserver.service launched on 33a92d68.../10.240.48.137
Unit kube-controller-manager.service launched on 33a92d68.../10.240.48.137
Unit kube-scheduler.service launched on 33a92d68.../10.240.48.137
Unit kube-register.service launched on 33a92d68.../10.240.48.137
Triggered global unit kube-kubelet.service start
Triggered global unit kube-proxy.service start

UNIT                             MACHINE                      ACTIVE       SUB
kube-apiserver.service           33a92d68.../10.240.48.137    active       running
kube-controller-manager.service  33a92d68.../10.240.48.137    active       running
kube-register.service            33a92d68.../10.240.48.137    activating   start-pre
kube-scheduler.service           33a92d68.../10.240.48.137    active       running

Kubernetes Cluster setup has finished !!!
```

6. Let's try access our Kubernetes cluster via `""`, which was copied to `~/k8s-cluster/bin` by the `1-bootstrap_cluster.sh` script.

   Type this in your terminal:

   $ cd ~/k8s-cluster/bin

   $ ./set_k8s_access.sh

   You should get an output similar to the following:

```
/coreos.com
/registry

UNIT                             MACHINE                      ACTIVE  SUB
kube-apiserver.service           33a92d68.../10.240.48.137    active  running
kube-controller-manager.service  33a92d68.../10.240.48.137    active  running
kube-kubelet.service             bf5d3a70.../10.240.235.6     active  running
kube-kubelet.service             fb67e5ec.../10.240.32.39     active  running
kube-proxy.service               bf5d3a70.../10.240.235.6     active  running
kube-proxy.service               fb67e5ec.../10.240.32.39     active  running
kube-register.service            33a92d68.../10.240.48.137    active  running
kube-scheduler.service           33a92d68.../10.240.48.137    active  running

NAME           LABELS                                 STATUS
10.240.235.6   kubernetes.io/hostname=10.240.235.6    Ready
10.240.32.39   kubernetes.io/hostname=10.240.32.39    Ready

Type exit when you are finished ...
```

As you can see, our Kubernetes cluster is up and running.

What `set_k8s_access.sh` does is that it provides `fleetctl` and `kubectl` with access to the remote `k8s-master` server by forwarding the `localhost` ports 2379 (`fleet`) and 8080 (Kubernetes master) to it.

1. Let's check out the Kubernetes cluster by typing this into the terminal:

   ```
   $ kubectl cluster-info
   ```

   You should see an output similar to this:

   ```
   Kubernetes master is running at http://localhost:8080
   ```

   Perfect! Now we can access the remote Kubernetes cluster from our local computer.

2. As we've got our Kubernetes cluster up and running, let's deploy the same `website1` Docker image that we used for our production cluster deployment.

   Type this into your terminal:

   ```
   $  kubectl run website1 --image=10.200.4.1:5000/website1
   --replicas=2 --port=80
   ```

   You should see the following output:

   ```
   CONTROLLER   CONTAINER(S)   IMAGE(S)                   SELECTOR       REPLICAS
   website1     website1       10.200.4.1:5000/website1   run=website1   2
   ```

   The previous command has created two `website1` pods listening on `port 80`. It has also created a replication controller named `website1`, and this replication controller ensures that there are always two pods running.

   We can list created `pods` by typing the following into your terminal:

   ```
   $ kubectl get pods
   ```

   You should see an output like this:

   ```
   NAME             READY   REASON    RESTARTS   AGE
   website1-82yqs   1/1     Running   0          5m
   website1-fa8tp   1/1     Running   0          5m
   ```

To list the created replication controller, type this into your terminal:

```
$ kubectl get rc
```

You should see the following output:

```
CONTROLLER   CONTAINER(S)   IMAGE(S)                      SELECTOR        REPLICAS
website1     website1       10.200.4.1:5000/website1      run=website1    2
```

3. Now, let's expose our pods to the Internet. The `Kubectl` command can integrate with the Google Compute Engine to add a public IP address for the `pods`. To do this, type the following line into your terminal:

   ```
   $ kubectl expose rc website1 --port=80 --type=LoadBalancer
   ```

   You should see an output like this:

   ```
   NAME       LABELS         SELECTOR       IP(S)    PORT(S)
   website1   run=website1   run=website1            80/TCP
   ```

   The previous command created a service named `website1` and mapped an external IP address to the service. To find that IP address, type this into your terminal:

   ```
   $ kubectl get services
   ```

   You should see an output similar to the following:

```
NAME         LABELS                                      SELECTOR       IP(S)            PORT(S)
kubernetes   component=apiserver,provider=kubernetes     <none>         10.100.0.1       443/TCP
website1     run=website1                                run=website1   10.100.156.59    80/TCP
                                                                        104.155.12.159
```

The IP in the bottom line is our IP, and it is of the load balancer. It is assigned to the `k8s-node-1` and `k8snode-2` servers and used by `website1` service.

Let's type this IP into our web browser. We should get an output similar to this:

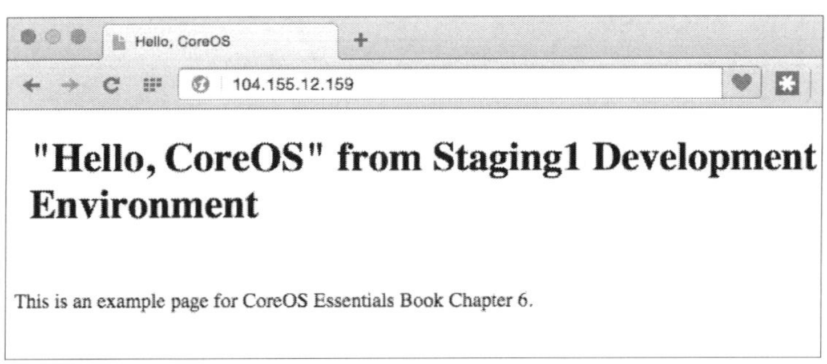

As you have seen previously, it shows exactly the same web page as we got on our production web servers. Also, it is exactly the same code as we had in the staging environment. We built the Docker image from it and used that Docker image for deployment on our production cluster and the Kubernetes cluster.

If you want, you can easily run more replicas of pods by using this simple command:

```
$ kubectl scale --replicas=4 rc website1
```

Let's check our replication controller by typing the following into our terminal:

```
$ kubectl get rc
```

You should see an output similar to this:

```
CONTROLLER   CONTAINER(S)   IMAGE(S)                     SELECTOR       REPLICAS
website1     website1       10.200.4.1:5000/website1     run=website1   4
```

The previous command scales the pods, and replication controller ensures that we always have four of them running.

> You can find plenty of usage examples to play with at `https://github.com/GoogleCloudPlatform/kubernetes/tree/master/examples`.

This book is too short to cover all the good things you can do with Kubernetes, but we should be seeing more Kubernetes books pop up soon.

> Some other URLs to look at are given here:
>
> If you are a Mac user, you can install one of the apps that will set your Kubernetes cluster on your Mac: 1 master x 2 nodes on `https://github.com/rimusz/coreos-osx-gui-kubernetes-cluster`, and standalone master/node on `https://github.com/rimusz/coreos-osx-gui-kubernetes-solo`.
>
> Other guides to Kubernetes on CoreOS are available at `https://github.com/GoogleCloudPlatform/kubernetes/blob/master/docs/getting-started-guides/coreos.md`.

Tectonic – CoreOS and Kubernetes combined for a commercial implementation

Tectonic (`http://tectonic.com`) is a commercial CoreOS distribution with a combined CoreOS and Kubernetes stack. It can be used by businesses of any size.

Tectonic is prepackaged with all the open source components of CoreOS and Kubernetes, and adds some more commercial features:

- Management console/UI for workflows and dashboards
- Corporate SSO integration
- Quay-integrated container registry for building and sharing Linux containers
- Tools for automation of container deployments
- Customized rolling updates

It can run in public clouds or on-premise.

Its management console is simple and easy to use:

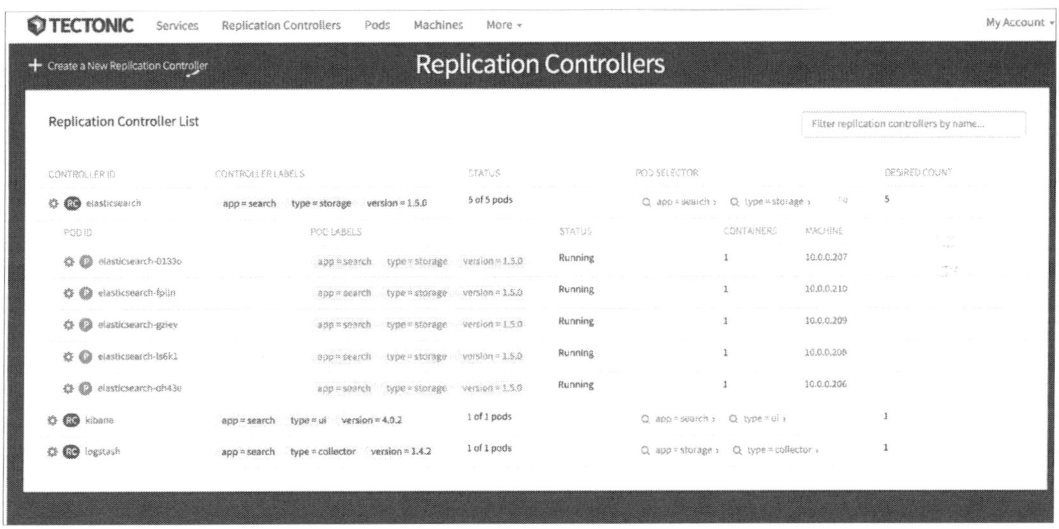

In the preceding screenshot, we have a visualization of our **Replication controllers** (**RC**). On the left-hand side, you can' see each RC with the labels will assign to pods as they're instantiated. Below the name of the RC, you'll see a list of all running pods that match the same label queries.

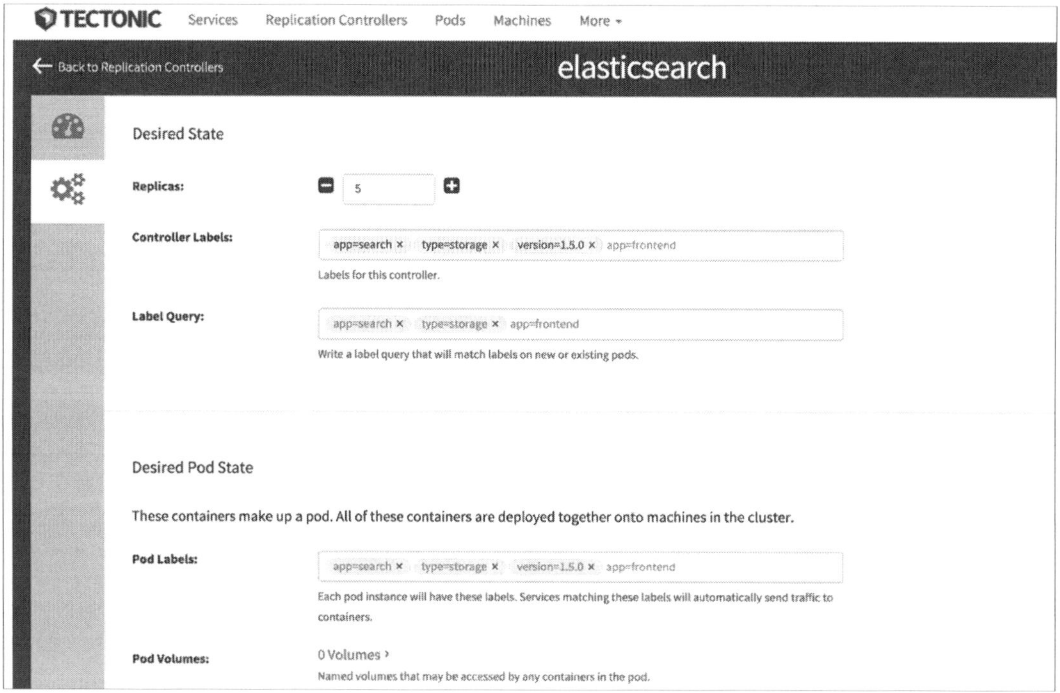

The preceding screenshot shows us the **elasticsearch** replication controller state, which labels are used there, and pod volumes.

Tectonic aims to provide an easily container deployment solution, and companies can begin seeing its benefits very quickly of using containers in enterprise.

Summary

In this chapter, we overviewed Google Kubernetes and covered what is about, its main components, and its CoreOS commercial implementation.

We hope that this book will equip you with all the information you need to leverage the power of CoreOS and the related containers, and help you develop effective computing networks. Thank you for reading it!

Index

A

C

D

[PACKT] open source
PUBLISHING
community experience distilled

Thank you for buying
CoreOS Essentials

About Packt Publishing

Packt, pronounced 'packed', published its first book, *Mastering phpMyAdmin for Effective MySQL Management*, in April 2004, and subsequently continued to specialize in publishing highly focused books on specific technologies and solutions.

Our books and publications share the experiences of your fellow IT professionals in adapting and customizing today's systems, applications, and frameworks. Our solution-based books give you the knowledge and power to customize the software and technologies you're using to get the job done. Packt books are more specific and less general than the IT books you have seen in the past. Our unique business model allows us to bring you more focused information, giving you more of what you need to know, and less of what you don't.

Packt is a modern yet unique publishing company that focuses on producing quality, cutting-edge books for communities of developers, administrators, and newbies alike. For more information, please visit our website at `www.packtpub.com`.

About Packt Open Source

In 2010, Packt launched two new brands, Packt Open Source and Packt Enterprise, in order to continue its focus on specialization. This book is part of the Packt Open Source brand, home to books published on software built around open source licenses, and offering information to anybody from advanced developers to budding web designers. The Open Source brand also runs Packt's Open Source Royalty Scheme, by which Packt gives a royalty to each open source project about whose software a book is sold.

Writing for Packt

We welcome all inquiries from people who are interested in authoring. Book proposals should be sent to `author@packtpub.com`. If your book idea is still at an early stage and you would like to discuss it first before writing a formal book proposal, then please contact us; one of our commissioning editors will get in touch with you.

We're not just looking for published authors; if you have strong technical skills but no writing experience, our experienced editors can help you develop a writing career, or simply get some additional reward for your expertise.

[PACKT] open source
community experience distilled
PUBLISHING

Learning Chef

ISBN: 978-1-78328-521-1 Paperback: 316 pages

Automate your infrastructure into code and leverage DevOps with Chef

1. Leverage the power of Chef to transform your infrastructure into code to deploy new features in minutes.
2. Understand the Chef architecture and its various components including the different types of server setups.
3. Packed with practical examples and industry best practices for real-world situations.

Mastering Wireless Penetration Testing for Highly Secured Environments

ISBN: 978-1-78216-318-3 Paperback: 220 pages

Scan, exploit, and crack wireless networks by using the most advanced techniques from security professionals

1. Conduct a full wireless penetration test and implement defensive techniques that can be used to protect wireless systems.
2. Crack WEP, WPA, and even WPA2 wireless networks.
3. A hands-on guide teaching how to expose wireless security threats through the eyes of an attacker.

Please check **www.PacktPub.com** for information on our titles

[PACKT] open source
PUBLISHING
community experience distilled

Mastering Gephi Network Visualization

ISBN: 978-1-78398-734-4   Paperback: 378 pages

Produce advanced network graphs in Gephi and gain valuable insights into your network datasets

1. Build sophisticated interactive network graphs using advanced Gephi layout features.
2. Master Gephi statistical and filtering techniques to easily navigate through even the densest network graphs.
3. An easy-to-follow guide introducing you to Gephi's advanced features, with step-by-step instructions and lots of examples.

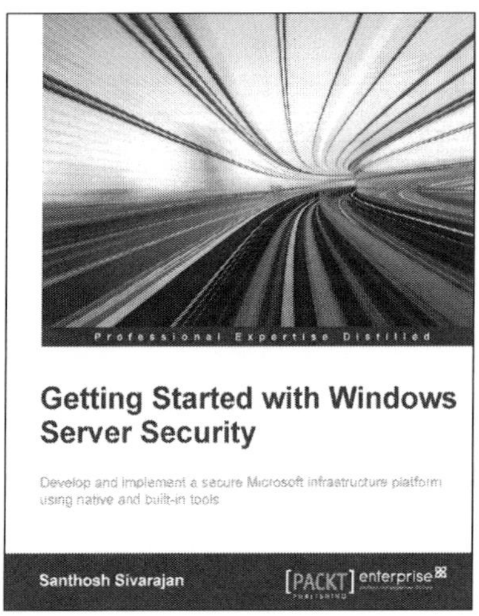

Getting Started with Windows Server Security

ISBN: 978-1-78439-872-9   Paperback: 240 pages

Develop and implement a secure Microsoft infrastructure platform using native and built-in tools

1. Learn how to identify and mitigate security risks in your Microsoft Server infrastructure.
2. Develop a proactive approach to common security threats to prevent sensitive data leakage and unauthorized access.
3. Step-by-step tutorial that provides real-world scenarios and security solutions.

Please check **www.PacktPub.com** for information on our titles

14113313R00076

Printed in Poland
by Amazon Fulfillment
Poland Sp. z o.o., Wrocław